Col...

COBUILD

Key Words for

WITHDRAWN

Finance

HarperCollins Publishers
Westerhill Road
Bishopbriggs
Glasgow
G64 2QT

First Edition 2013

Reprint 10 9 8 7 6 5 4 3 2 1 0

© HarperCollins Publishers 2013

ISBN 978-0-00-748984-8

Collins® and COBUILD® are
registered trademarks of
HarperCollins Publishers Limited

www.collinslanguage.com

A catalogue record for this book is
available from the British Library

CD recorded by Networks SRL,
Milan, Italy

Typeset by Davidson Publishing
Solutions, Glasgow

Printed in Great Britain by Clays Ltd,
St Ives plc

Acknowledgements
We would like to thank those authors
and publishers who kindly gave
permission for copyright material
to be used in the Collins Corpus.
We would also like to thank Times
Newspapers Ltd for providing
valuable data.

Contents

Contributors

Specialist consultant
Mariette Knoblauch, Chartered Professional Accountant,
Ballard Beancounters, Seattle USA

Project manager
Patrick White

Editors
Katherine Carroll
Ros Combley
Kate Mohideen
Enid Pearsons
Elizabeth Walter
Kate Woodford

Computing support
Mark Taylor

For the publisher
Gerry Breslin
Lucy Cooper
Kerry Ferguson
Gavin Gray
Elaine Higgleton
Persephone Lock
Ruth O'Donovan
Rosie Pearce
Lisa Sutherland

Introduction

Collins COBUILD Key Words for Finance is a brand-new vocabulary book for students who want to master the English of Finance in order to study or work in the field. This title contains the 500 most important English words and phrases relating to Finance, as well as a range of additional features which have been specially designed to help you to *really* understand and use the language of this specific area.

The main body of the book contains alphabetically organized dictionary-style entries for the key words and phrases of Finance. These vocabulary items have been specially chosen to fully prepare you for the type of language that you will need in this field. Many are specialized terms that are very specific to this profession and area of study. Others are more common or general words and phrases that are often used in the context of Finance.

Each word and phrase is explained clearly and precisely, in English that is easy to understand. In addition, each entry is illustrated with examples taken from the Collins Corpus. Of course, you will also find grammatical information about the way that the words and phrases behave.

In amongst the alphabetically organized entries, you will find valuable word-building features that will help you gain a better understanding of this area of English. For example, some features provide extra help with tricky pronunciations, while others pull together groups of related words that can usefully be learned as a set.

At the start of this book you will see lists of words and phrases, helpfully organized by topic area. You can use these lists to revise sets of vocabulary and to prepare for writing tasks. You will also find with this book an MP3 CD, containing a recording of each headword in the book, followed by an example sentence. This will help you to learn and remember pronunciations of words and phrases. Furthermore, the exercise section at the end of this book gives you an opportunity to memorize important words and phrases, to assess what you have learned, and to work out which areas still need attention.

So whether you are studying Finance, or you are already working in the field and intend to improve your career prospects, we are confident that *Collins COBUILD Key Words for Finance* will equip you for success in the future.

Guide to Dictionary Entries

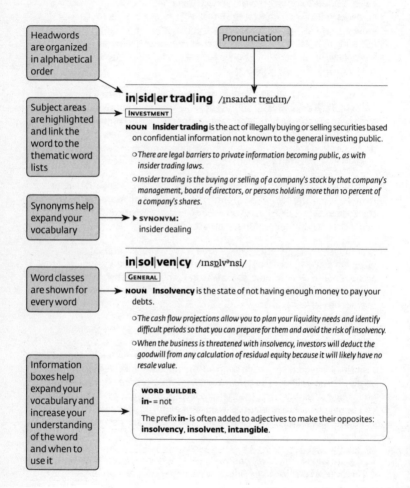

Headwords are organized in alphabetical order

Pronunciation

Subject areas are highlighted and link the word to the thematic word lists

Synonyms help expand your vocabulary

Word classes are shown for every word

Information boxes help expand your vocabulary and increase your understanding of the word and when to use it

in|sid|er trad|ing /ɪnsaɪdər treɪdɪŋ/

INVESTMENT

NOUN **Insider trading** is the act of illegally buying or selling securities based on confidential information not known to the general investing public.

○ There are legal barriers to private information becoming public, as with insider trading laws.

○ Insider trading is the buying or selling of a company's stock by that company's management, board of directors, or persons holding more than 10 percent of a company's shares.

▶ SYNONYM:
insider dealing

in|sol|ven|cy /ɪnsɒlvᵊnsi/

GENERAL

NOUN **Insolvency** is the state of not having enough money to pay your debts.

○ The cash flow projections allow you to plan your liquidity needs and identify difficult periods so that you can prepare for them and avoid the risk of insolvency.

○ When the business is threatened with insolvency, investors will deduct the goodwill from any calculation of residual equity because it will likely have no resale value.

> **WORD BUILDER**
> **in-** = not
>
> The prefix **in-** is often added to adjectives to make their opposites:
> **insolvency, insolvent, intangible**.

Guide to Dictionary Entries

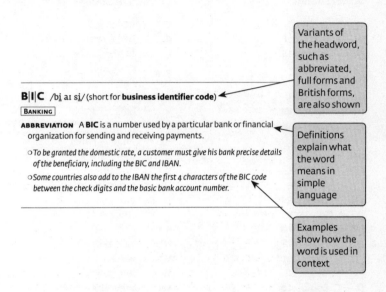

B|I|C /ˌbiː aɪ siː/ (short for **business identifier code**)

Variants of the headword, such as abbreviated, full forms and British forms, are also shown

BANKING

ABBREVIATION A **BIC** is a number used by a particular bank or financial organization for sending and receiving payments.

Definitions explain what the word means in simple language

○ To be granted the domestic rate, a customer must give his bank precise details of the beneficiary, including the BIC and IBAN.

○ Some countries also add to the IBAN the first 4 characters of the BIC code between the check digits and the basic bank account number.

Examples show how the word is used in context

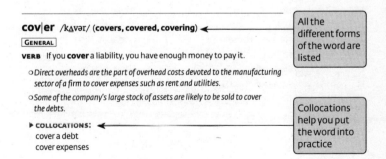

cov|er /kʌvər/ (covers, covered, covering)

All the different forms of the word are listed

GENERAL

VERB If you **cover** a liability, you have enough money to pay it.

○ Direct overheads are the part of overhead costs devoted to the manufacturing sector of a firm to cover expenses such as rent and utilities.

○ Some of the company's large stock of assets are likely to be sold to cover the debts.

▶ COLLOCATIONS:
cover a debt
cover expenses

Collocations help you put the word into practice

Guide to Pronunciation Symbols

Vowel Sounds

ɑ	calm, ah
ɑr	heart, far
æ	act, mass
ɑɪ	dive, cry
ɑɪər	fire, tire
ɑʊ	out, down
ɑʊər	flour, sour
ɛ	met, lend, pen
eɪ	say, weight
ɛər	fair, care
ɪ	fit, win
i	feed, me
ɪər	near, beard
ɒ	lot, spot
oʊ	note, coat
ɔ	claw, bought
ɔr	more, cord
ɔɪ	boy, joint
ʊ	could, stood
u	you, use
ʊər	lure, endure
ɜr	turn, third
ʌ	fund, must
ə	*the first vowel in* about
ər	*the first vowel in* forgotten
i	*the second vowel in* very
u	*the second vowel in* actual

Consonant Sounds

b	bed, rub
d	done, red
f	fit, if
g	good, dog
h	hat, horse
y	yellow, you
k	king, pick
l	lip, bill
ᵊl	handle, panel
m	mat, ram
n	not, tin
ᵊn	hidden, written
p	pay, lip
r	run, read
s	soon, bus
t	talk, bet
v	van, love
w	win, wool
ʍ	why, wheat
z	zoo, buzz
ʃ	ship, wish
ʒ	measure, leisure
ŋ	sing, working
tʃ	cheap, witch
θ	thin, myth
ð	then, other
dʒ	joy, bridge

Word Lists

BANKING

ABA
ACH
APR
APY
bank account
bank draft
banker's acceptance
BIC
BIS
bridge loan
cashier's check
CD
certified check
checking account
CHIPS
clearing
commercial bank
correspondent bank
credit union
custodian bank
cutoff time
direct debit
direct deposit
discount rate
ECB
EFT
electronic check conversion
endorse
escheat
FDIC
federal funds rate
Federal Reserve
Fedwire
finance charge
fixed rate
FRB
frozen account
hold
IBAN
interbank rate
investment bank
joint account
letter of credit
LIBOR
lockbox
LTV
MICR encoding
national bank
NCUA
nostro account
NSF
outstanding

payday loan
periodic rate
PIN
postdate
prime rate
principal
reserve
RTGS
RTN
run on a bank
safe deposit box
savings account
savings and loan
secured
stop payment
SWIFT
time deposit
void
vostro account
wire transfer

Credit

adverse action
balance transfer
closed-end loan
collateral
credit bureau
credit rating
credit risk
credit score
debt covenant
debt relief
demand note
FICO
line of credit
merchant account
open-ended loan
overlimit
prime
teaser rate
unsecured

CORPORATE

acquisition
all-cash deal
annual report
antitrust
asset-stripping
balance sheet
black knight
board of directors
bolt-on
book value

bootstrap
bottom line
breakeven
break even
buy out
capital account
capital employed
capital expenditure
C corporation
corporation
debt restructuring
demutualization
disinvest
dividend cover
EBITDA
equity
financial statements
fiscal year
free cash flow
GAAP
go bust
going concern
golden parachute
goodwill
holding company
hostile takeover
income statement
interim results
international accounting
    standards
LBO
leverage
limited partnership
LLC
LLP
mark-to-market
merger
paid-in capital
partnership
poison pill
profit margin
profit warning
pro forma
retained earnings
revenue stream
sales revenue
S corporation
sinking fund
spin off
statement of cash flows
statement of earnings and
    comprehensive income
subsidiary

transfer pricing
treasury stock
windfall profits
working capital

Accounting
debt-to-equity ratio

ECONOMICS
bailout
balance of payments
boom
boom-bust cycle
bubble
bust
demand curve
diminishing returns
discounted cash flow
efficient frontier
forecast
GDP
GNP
government deficit
inflation
lagging indicator
leading indicator
money supply
NAFTA
national debt
OCC
opportunity cost
present value of future cash flows
recession
seigniorage
sovereign debt
sunk cost
Treasury
usury
yield curve

FOREIGN EXCHANGE
convertible currency
cross rate
devaluation
devalue
Eurodollars
exchange rate
fixed exchange rate
floating rate
forex
forward rate
functional currency
gain on translation

hard currency
loss on translation
peg
soft currency
spot rate
translation

GENERAL
afloat
allocation
amortize
appraisal
arbitration
arrears
backdate
bad debt
bankruptcy
bill of exchange
bonus
capital
capitalization
capitalize
capital lease
cash flow
certified public accountant
COD
compound interest
counteroffer
cover
default
depreciation
divest
escrow
exposure
factoring
fair market value
fiduciary
financial instrument
front-end
IMF
impairment
insolvency
insolvent
installment sales
intangible
intellectual property
interest
interest rate
internal rate of return
invoice
lease-back
lease with option to buy
liquid assets

liquidity
negotiable
note payable
offer
proceeds
promissory note
pro rata
real property
residual
retroactive
Sallie Mae
terms of payment
title
valuation
voucher

INVESTMENT
arbitrage
back-end load
basis point
blind trust
bond
bondholder
bottom fishing
capital gains
capital loss
closed-end fund
commercial paper
commodity
contango
convertible
cost of capital
coupon rate
credit swap
current yield
CUSIP number
dealer
debenture
debt swap
derivative
discretionary trust
disinvest
diversification
dollar cost averaging
ETF
forward contracts
fund
fund manager
futures
gain on sale
hedge
hedge fund
index

insider trading
interest rate swap
in the money
invest
investment
ISIN
joint venture
junk bonds
ladder
loss on sale
maturity
money market
muni bonds
mutual fund
net present value
no-load
par value
piggyback investing
premium
rate of return
redeem
return of capital
return on assets
return on capital
return on equity
return on investment
securities
speculation
spot market
spot price
spread
stalking horse
standing settlement instructions
straddle
surrender
swap
swaption
T-bill
T-bond
tender offer
tracker
trust account
underwrite
unit trust
unload
US Savings bond
weighted average cost of capital
white knight
yield
yield to maturity
zero-coupon bonds

Retirement
401(k)
annuity
IRA
pension fund
Roth IRA

Stocks
above par
accredited investor
aftermarket
Amex
ask
at par
backwardation
bear
bear market
bear raid
below par
bid
Big Board
blue-chip
bonus issue
book value
break-up value
broker
brokerage account
bull
bull market
buy forward
buy out
call
capital stock
cash-in-lieu
clearing house
close out
commission
common stock
CSO
cum dividend
cumulative
dilution
distribution
dividend
earnings per share
ESOP
ex dividend
ex-dividend date
exercise price
face value
go long
issue price
large-cap

make a market
margin
margin call
marketable securities
market cap
mid-cap
NASDAQ
NYSE
option
out of the money
over-the-counter
par
peg
penny stocks
portfolio
preferred stock
price earnings ratio
private placement
prospectus
proxy
public company
put
quote
RSU
SEC
selloff
sell short
serial bonds
settle
settlement agent
settlement date
settlement price
share
share capital
share certificate
shareholder
shareholders' equity
share repurchase
small-cap
SOX
stock
stock dividend
stock options
stock split
stock symbol
stock warrant
strike price
ticker
vesting
wash sale

Venture capitalism
angel
backer
backing
bootstrap
burn rate
corporate venturing
direct public offering
first-round financing
float
initial public offering
liquidity event
ramen profitable
seed capital
seed money
startup
sweat equity
term sheet
venture capital
venture capitalist

Mortgage
ARM
balloon mortgage
balloon payment
CDO
conventional mortgage
Fannie Mae
foreclosure
Freddie Mac
Ginnie Mae
HELOC
lien
modification
PITI
PMI
redlining
refinance
reverse mortgage
subordinated
subprime loan
tranche
underwater

TAX
ad valorem
customs duty
tax haven
tax holiday
tax shelter

A–Z

Aa

4|0|1|(k) /fɔr oʊ wʌn keɪ/ **(401(k)s)**

INVESTMENT: RETIREMENT

NOUN A **401(k)** is a type of retirement account.

- ○ Also contributing to job growth is the widespread popularity of defined contribution pension plans such as 401(k) plans.
- ○ There are serious issues with 401(k)s that prevent many of these plans from delivering promised or expected retirement benefits.

A|B|A /eɪ bi eɪ/ (short for **American Bankers Association**)

BANKING

ABBREVIATION The **ABA** is a professional organization that represents US banks and other financial institutions.

- ○ The ABA has lobbied long and hard for involuntary taxpayer financial support and additional bank tax breaks.
- ○ The money had not been transferred because no one at the branch knew the ABA code for the branch in Texas.

PRONUNCIATION

Three-letter abbreviations are usually pronounced as separate letters with the main stress on the last syllable.

ABA /eɪ bi eɪ/
CDO /si di oʊ/
FRB /ɛf ar bi/
RSU /ar ɛs yu/

A

a|bove par /əbʌv pɑr/

INVESTMENT: STOCKS

ADJECTIVE If a bond or stock is priced **above par**, it is trading for more than its face value.

○ *The notes will be offered at various prices above par to bring the yield down to market rates.*

○ *If prices are above par, the bond is priced at greater than 100, which is called trading at a premium.*

▶ **COLLOCATIONS:**
  be priced above par
  trade above par

RELATED WORDS

If a bond or stock is priced **below par**, it is trading below its face value. If a bond or stock is priced **at par**, it is trading at its face value.

---

ac|cred|it|ed in|ves|tor /əkrɛdɪtɪd ɪnvɛstər/ (**accredited investors**)

INVESTMENT: STOCKS

NOUN An **accredited investor** is an organization or a wealthy individual that is considered to be financially knowledgeable, and can buy securities that are not registered with the SEC.

○ *Each purchaser who is not an accredited investor must have the knowledge and experience in finance and business to be capable of evaluating the merits and risks of the prospective investment.*

○ *An accredited investor is a wealthy investor with a net worth of at least $7 million or more than $200,000 in gross annual income.*

A|C|H /eɪ si eɪtʃ/ (short for **Automated Clearing House**)

BANKING

ABBREVIATION The **ACH** is an electronic network used by member institutions to process financial transactions between banks in the US.

○*ACH payments are used for both business and retail payments as an electronic alternative to checks.*

○*Many shareholders have their dividend payments made through ACH directly into their personal accounts.*

ac|qui|si|tion /ækwɪzɪʃⁿn/

CORPORATE

NOUN An **acquisition** is the act of buying another company or part of a company.

○*The company has said it will now explore other opportunities for expansion, and it is expected to use the proceeds from the deal to help finance another acquisition.*

○*A management buyout is the acquisition of a company by its management team, assisted by external or other financing.*

ad va|lo|rem /æd vəlɔrəm/

TAX

ADJECTIVE An **ad valorem** tax is charged at the estimated value of the goods being taxed. It comes from the Latin, meaning "according to value."

○*Motor vehicle ad valorem tax is based on the assessed value of the vehicle.*

○*As prices inflate, so will tax revenues, since most rates are ad valorem.*

ad|verse ac|tion /ædvɜrs ækʃən/

BANKING: CREDIT

NOUN An **adverse action** notice is an official explanation by a financial institution of why they are refusing to grant credit to someone.

○*In cases of adverse action, consumers will be notified by the bank as to the reasons for the refusal.*

○*You have the right to know when an adverse action was taken based on information contained in a credit report.*

A

a|float /əflˈoʊt/

GENERAL

ADVERB If a person, a business, or a country stays **afloat**, they have just enough money to pay their debts and continue operating.

  ○ *A number of efforts were being made to keep the company afloat.*

  ○ *Depending on the economy, the company may be under tremendous pressure to stay afloat, or it may have great opportunities for growth.*

▶ **COLLOCATIONS:**
keep afloat
remain afloat
stay afloat

---

af|ter|mar|ket /ˈæftərmɑrkɪt/ (aftermarkets)

INVESTMENT: STOCKS

NOUN The **aftermarket** is the buying and selling of stocks and bonds after they have been issued.

  ○ *The period after a new issue is initially sold to the public is referred to as the aftermarket.*

  ○ *For the primary market to thrive, there must be an aftermarket that provides liquidity for the investment security where holders of securities can sell them to other investors for cash.*

---

all-cash deal /ɔl kæʃ dil/ (all-cash deals)

CORPORATE

NOUN An **all-cash deal** is a financial transaction in which the payment is made entirely in money.

  ○ *In an all-cash deal, the acquiring company typically pays the target company's shareholders a fixed price per share in cash.*

  ○ *Shareholders are entitled to demand an all-cash deal.*

---

al|lo|ca|tion /ˌæləkeɪʃ°n/

GENERAL

NOUN An **allocation** is an amount of money that is given to a particular person or used for a particular purpose.

○ If any of the committees doesn't meet its reduction target, its budget allocation would be cut across the board.

○ Start-of-the-year allocations made by foreign institutional investors can explain only part of the boom.

Am|ex /ˈæmɛks/

INVESTMENT: STOCKS

NOUN **Amex** is the second-largest stock exchange in the US, after the New York Stock Exchange.

○ The Amex Index climbed 2.66 to 372.78, topping the previous high of 372.40, set last Wednesday.

○ On the Amex, the company was the volume leader, although short interest edged down 0.2 percent to 3.67 million shares.

---

a|mor|tize /ˈæmərtaɪz/ (amortizes, amortized, amortizing)

GENERAL

VERB If you **amortize** a debt, you pay it back in regular payments.

○ There's little advantage to amortizing the loan, especially on a 30 or 40-year basis.

○ Although the premium is being earned gradually over the policy period, the initial acquisition and underwriting expenses cannot be amortized over the same period.

---

an|gel /ˈeɪndʒəl/ (angels)

INVESTMENT: VENTURE CAPITALISM

NOUN An **angel** is an investor who uses their own funds to provide capital for a startup.

○ Venture capitalists will not touch the space industry but, increasingly, angel investors are playing a role.

○ A business angel can provide both finance and business expertise to an investee company.

A

an|nu|al re|port /ˈænyuəl rɪpɔrt/ (**annual reports**)

CORPORATE

NOUN An **annual report** is a report that the directors of a company present to its stockholders each year.

- ○ *The financial statement section of our most recent annual report is 32 pages long.*
- ○ *The annual report tells you what the company did last year, and how good its financial management was.*

an|nu|i|ty /əˈnuɪti/ (**annuities**)

INVESTMENT: RETIREMENT

NOUN An **annuity** is a life insurance contract that is usually sold as a retirement investment.

- ○ *An annuity is a tax-deferred retirement savings plan that resembles an individual retirement account.*
- ○ *If they sell their rental property, they may want to purchase an annuity with some of the funds in order to replace the fixed income they were receiving in rent.*

an|ti|trust /ˈæntitrʌst/

CORPORATE

ADJECTIVE Antitrust activities are illegal activities that unfairly reduce competition, such as price-fixing, monopolies, and restraint of trade.

- ○ *The Department of Justice automatically reviews all bids over a certain size for antitrust and other public-policy implications.*
- ○ *Many forms of collusion are violations of US antitrust laws.*

ap|prais|al /əˈpreɪzəl/ (**appraisals**)

GENERAL

NOUN An **appraisal** is a professional examination of real or personal property to determine its market value.

- ○ *An independent appraisal of the company's real estate holdings values those assets at about $1.1 billion.*
- ○ *The company commissioned appraisals of the land value, and the timber value.*

a

A|P|R /eɪ pi ɑr/ (short for **annual percentage rate**)

BANKING

ABBREVIATION **APR** is the annual cost of a loan, including interest, insurance, and the original fee.

- ○ *Shoppers with store credit cards could be paying an APR of as much as 30 percent.*
- ○ *Interest on the 9-month marketing loan has a current rate at 3.125 percent APR.*

A|P|Y /eɪ pi waɪ/ (short for **annual percentage yield**)

BANKING

ABBREVIATION **APY** is the annual rate of return on an investment.

- ○ *The APY makes it easy to compare rates among financial institutions.*
- ○ *The APY is the rate actually earned or paid in one year, taking into account the effect of compounding.*

ar|bi|trage /ɑrbɪtrɑʒ/

INVESTMENT

NOUN **Arbitrage** is the simultaneous purchase and sale of an asset in order to take advantage of a difference in price.

- ○ *A dealer who can ease a billion dollars of highly volatile long-term bonds into his own portfolio and hedge it discreetly through arbitrage often captures the business of coveted accounts.*
- ○ *Arbitrage takes advantage of discrepancies in price or yields in different markets.*

ar|bi|tra|tion /ɑrbɪtreɪʃən/

GENERAL

NOUN **Arbitration** is a process for settling a dispute by agreeing to let an impartial third party make a decision, outside of the legal court system.

- ○ *Many brokers refuse to do business with investors who decline to sign statements agreeing to settle disputes only through arbitration, and not in court.*
- ○ *Usually, when you open a brokerage account, you sign an agreement to use arbitration to resolve any possible future disputes.*

A

ARM /ɑrm/ (short for **adjustable rate mortgage**)

MORTGAGE

ABBREVIATION **ARM** is a type of mortgage where the interest rate may change according to changes in other rates.

○ *The discounted introductory rate on an ARM linked to the one-year Treasury bill, a commonly used index, was 11.96 percent.*

○ *With an ARM, the interest rate can fluctuate based on a stated index during a stated time period, typically with a low initial rate.*

ar|rears /əriərz/

GENERAL

NOUN If sums of money are paid **in arrears**, they are paid at the end of a period of time.

○ *Interest is paid in arrears, after you use the money.*

○ *An annuity in arrears is an annuity with a first payment one full period hence, rather than immediately.*

▶ **COLLOCATION:**
pay in arrears

ask /æsk/

INVESTMENT: STOCKS

NOUN The **ask** is the price at which someone is willing to sell stocks or property in auction.

○ *Dealers quote two premiums on each contract, with the bid being what buyers are willing to pay, and the ask being what sellers want to be paid.*

○ *The market maker usually buys the stock at the bid price, hoping to sell it later at the ask price and earn the difference.*

as|set-strip|ping /æset strɪpɪŋ/

CORPORATE

NOUN **Asset-stripping** is the act of buying companies cheaply, selling their assets to make a profit, and then closing the companies down.

○ *The firm was accused of asset-stripping after it sold off its wholesale business.*

○ When the assets of the company are sold off for making quick profit instead of running the company for steady and long-term gain, asset-stripping is said to have occurred.

---

at par /æt pɑr/

INVESTMENT: STOCKS

ADJECTIVE If a bond or stock is priced **at par**, it is trading at its face value.

○ The serial bonds are priced at par to yield from 6.30 percent in 2002 to 7 percent in 2012.

○ The bank holding company said the notes will be redeemed at par plus accrued interest.

▶ **COLLOCATIONS:**
be priced at par
trade at par

Bb

---

back|date /bǽkdeɪt/ (backdates, backdated, backdating)

GENERAL

VERB If a document or an arrangement is **backdated**, its effect starts from a date before the date when it is completed or signed.

○ *The contract that was signed on Thursday morning was backdated to March 11.*

○ *Speculators were betting that the government would raise its interest rate and backdate the increase.*

▶ **COLLOCATION:**
backdate a check

---

back-end load /bǽk ɛnd loʊd/ (back-end loads)

INVESTMENT

NOUN A **back-end load** is a charge that an investor pays when they sell shares in a mutual fund, or when they cancel a life insurance policy.

○ *A back-end load can amount to as much as 5 or 6 percent of the investment.*

○ *Some back-end load funds impose a full commission if the shares are redeemed within a designated length of time, such as one year.*

---

back|er /bǽkər/ (backers)

INVESTMENT: VENTURE CAPITALISM

NOUN A **backer** is someone who helps or supports a project, an organization, or a person, usually by giving money.

○ *I was looking for a backer to assist me in the attempted buyout.*

○ *Despite around $20m raised from backers, a steady stream of losses has left the company with only six months of cash reserves.*

back|ing /bækɪŋ/

INVESTMENT: VENTURE CAPITALISM

NOUN If someone has the **backing of** an organization or an important person, they receive support or money in order to do something.

○ The small company needed his advice to get financial backing and legal assistance.

○ The technical and financial backing of the joint venture will allow the global marketing of the company's textile dyes.

back|ward|a|tion /bækwərdeɪʃən/

INVESTMENT: STOCKS

NOUN **Backwardation** is a situation in which the price of a forward or futures contract is trading below the expected spot price when the contract matures.

○ Our test results show that the basis pattern of these futures will generally switch from backwardation several months before the last trading day to contango as it approaches the last trading day.

○ Copper, like oil, is an industrial commodity that gets used up, and can fall into backwardation.

bad debt /bæd dɛt/ (**bad debts**)

GENERAL

NOUN A **bad debt** is a sum of money that a person or company owes but is not likely to pay back.

○ The bank set aside 1.1 billion dollars to cover bad debts from business failures.

○ Bankruptcies have fallen sharply of late, which should slow the growth of bad debts on bank's books.

bail|out /beɪlaʊt/ (**bailouts**)

ECONOMICS

NOUN A **bailout** is the act of providing money to a company or a bank that is failing, in order to keep it from closing down.

○ A recession could mean huge losses at state-run factories, requiring a bailout from the state of billions of dollars.

○ *A bailout is a capital infusion offered to a business with a national or multinational footprint that is in danger of bankruptcy, insolvency, or total liquidation.*

---

bal|ance of pay|ments /bæləns əv peɪmənts/
ECONOMICS

NOUN A country's **balance of payments** is the difference, over a period of time, between the payments it makes to other countries for imports and the payments it receives from other countries for exports.

○ *Export and import data are adjusted to bring them in line with the requirements for compiling the nation's balance of payments.*

○ *The nation has the option of taking the gold out of economy, thus building up a hoard of gold and retaining its favorable balance of payments.*

---

bal|ance sheet /bæləns ʃit/ (balance sheets)
CORPORATE

NOUN A **balance sheet** is a statement of the amount of money and property that a company has and the amount of money that it owes.

○ *The strong currency has helped the balance sheets of Brazilian companies with international aspirations.*

○ *The company has improved its balance sheet during the past few years and begun making sizable payments to its underfunded pension-plan fund.*

---

bal|ance trans|fer /bæləns trænsfər/ (balance transfers)
BANKING: CREDIT

NOUN A **balance transfer** is the act of moving the amount of money that you owe from one credit card to another credit card that has a lower interest rate.

○ *If you find yourself paying a high interest rate on your existing credit cards, why not ask for a balance transfer to a new 0 percent credit card?*

○ *The rate of interest is substantial when borrowing on a credit card account, but banks frequently offer low balance transfer rates.*

bal|loon mort|gage /bəlun mɔrgɪdʒ/ (**balloon mortgages**)

MORTGAGE

NOUN A **balloon mortgage** is a mortgage in which you make small payments over a period of time and repay the balance in one large final payment.

○ They have made a down payment on a balloon mortgage that will require huge, escalating payments in the future.

○ A balloon mortgage for $25,000 has interest-only payments for 5 years at 12 percent, with the full principal of $25,000 due after 5 years.

bal|loon pay|ment /bəlun peɪmənt/ (**balloon payments**)

MORTGAGE

NOUN A **balloon payment** is a large final payment of a loan.

○ At the end of the five years, the loan will be due and payable and the investor will have a balloon payment to make.

○ One form of deferring principals is to make a balloon payment at the end of the term.

bank ac|count /bæŋk əkaʊnt/ (**bank accounts**)

BANKING

NOUN A **bank account** is an arrangement with a bank that allows you to keep your money in the bank and to take some out when you need it.

○ The loans were backed by letters of credit secured by deposits in Swiss bank accounts.

○ With point-of-sale debit cards, funds are electronically transferred out of a consumer's bank account at the time of purchase.

bank draft /bæŋk dræft/ (**bank drafts**)

BANKING

NOUN A **bank draft** is a check where the bank guarantees payment, or an automatic electronic payment from a bank account.

○ A bank draft is more likely to be accepted when purchasing goods abroad because the foreign exporter knows that even if the company purchasing the goods goes bankrupt, it will still be paid off.

B

○A bank draft is a promise of payment similar to a check that is issued by a firm, payable at some future date, and guaranteed for a fee by the bank that stamps it accepted.

---

bank|er's ac|cept|ance /bæŋkərz æksɛptəns/ (**banker's acceptances**)

BANKING

NOUN A **banker's acceptance** is a short-term negotiable financing instrument guaranteed by a bank.

○Institutional investors responded to declining money-market fund yields by shifting some assets out of funds and into direct money-market instruments like banker's acceptances.

○A banker's acceptance is a short-term credit investment created by a non-financial firm and guaranteed by a bank as to payment.

---

bank|rupt|cy¹ /bæŋkrʌptsi/

GENERAL

NOUN **Bankruptcy** is a legal recognition that a person, an organization, or a company does not have sufficient assets to repay its debts.

○It is the second airline in two months to file for bankruptcy.

○During bankruptcy, the debtor's assets are held and managed by a court appointed trustee.

> **TALKING ABOUT BANKRUPTCY**
>
> If someone starts the legal process to become bankrupt, they **file for** bankruptcy. To say they are bankrupt, they **declare** bankruptcy.
>
> If a person or organization is in danger of becoming bankrupt, they **face** or **risk** bankruptcy, or are **on the verge of** bankruptcy.
>
> If a person or organization manages not to become bankrupt, they **avoid**, **avert**, or **escape** bankruptcy.

bank|rupt|cy² /ˈbæŋkrʌptsi/ (**bankruptcies**)

GENERAL

NOUN A **bankruptcy** is when an organization or a person goes bankrupt.

○ *With the recession, the number of corporate bankruptcies climbed in August.*

○ *In the event of a bankruptcy, claims of junior creditors are satisfied only after the satisfaction of claims of senior creditors.*

ba|sis point /ˈbeɪsɪs pɔɪnt/ (**basis points**)

INVESTMENT

NOUN A **basis point** is one hundredth of a percent, used in expressing differences in interest rates.

○ *The dollar climbed about 30 basis points during the morning session.*

○ *In the bond market, the smallest measure used for quoting yields is a basis point.*

bear /bɛər/ (**bears**)

INVESTMENT: STOCKS

NOUN A **bear** is a person who sells shares of stock when they expect the price to drop, hoping to make a profit by buying the shares again after a short time.

○ *A bear believes the market will trend downward.*

○ *The bears expect the market to decline.*

bear mar|ket /bɛər ˈmɑrkɪt/ (**bear markets**)

INVESTMENT: STOCKS

NOUN A **bear market** is a situation in which people are selling a lot of shares of stock because they expect the price to drop, so that they can make a profit by buying the shares again after a short time.

○ *It takes more than just a big percentage fall for a bear market to be officially under way; the decline also needs to be long-lasting.*

○ *In a bear market, prices are usually low.*

bear raid /bɛər reɪd/ (bear raids)

INVESTMENT: STOCKS

NOUN A **bear raid** is an attempt to force down the price of a stock by selling many shares or by spreading a negative rumor about the company that owns it.

○ *A bear raid is an attempt by investors to manipulate the price of a stock by selling large numbers of shares short.*

○ *Hong Kong's government is to sell blue-chip stocks worth HK$225 billion that it acquired when it was trying to stop a bear raid on the market.*

be|low par /bɪloʊ pɑr/

INVESTMENT: STOCKS

ADJECTIVE If a bond or stock is priced **below par**, it is trading below its face value.

○ *If a bond is priced below par, it is trading at a discount.*

○ *The issuing company promised not to issue further shares below par, so investors could be confident that no one else was receiving a more favorable issue price.*

▶ **COLLOCATIONS:**
 be priced below par
 trade below par

B|I|C /bi aɪ si/ (short for **business identifier code**)

BANKING

ABBREVIATION A **BIC** is a number used by a particular bank or financial organization for sending and receiving payments.

○ *To be granted the domestic rate, a customer must give his bank precise details of the beneficiary, including the BIC and IBAN.*

○ *Some countries also add to the IBAN the first 4 characters of the BIC code between the check digits and the basic bank account number.*

bid /bɪd/ (bids)

INVESTMENT: STOCKS

NOUN The **bid** is the price that investors are willing to pay for a particular security.

○ Investors feel that the bid price undervalues the company.

○ Dealers are said to make a market when they quote bid and offered prices at which they stand ready to buy and sell.

Big Board /bɪg bɔrd/

INVESTMENT: STOCKS

NOUN The **Big Board** is a name for the New York Stock Exchange. This nickname for the New York Stock Exchange comes from the large display board there that shows stock prices.

○ The New York Stock Exchange is sometimes called the Big Board, a reference to a blackboard that was used to post the prices of securities.

○ Advancing issues on the Big Board were ahead of decliners.

---

bill of ex|change (ABBR **BOE**) /bɪl əv ɪkstʃeɪndʒ/ (**bills of exchange**)

GENERAL

NOUN A **bill of exchange** is a document ordering someone to pay someone else a stated sum of money at a future date.

○ The actual payment will be made by means of a bill of exchange, and this will be drawn up by the exporter or the exporter's bank after the receipt of the credit advice.

○ The lender draws up a bill of exchange for a specified sum of money payable at a given future date.

B|I|S /bi aɪ ɛs/ (short for **Bank for International Settlements**)

BANKING

ABBREVIATION The **BIS** is an institution that promotes international financial cooperation and serves as a bank for all central banks.

○ The BIS standards will require banks to have capital roughly equal to 8 percent of their total assets.

○ The BIS says that banks only need to hold twice as much capital against loans to commercial-property projects as against mortgages.

black knight /blæk naɪt/ (black knights)

CORPORATE

NOUN A **black knight** is someone making an unwelcome takeover attempt of a company, especially with the intention of selling it off or breaking it up into different organizations.

○ A black knight is a firm that launches an unwelcome and contested takeover bid for some other firm.

○ The company has a preplanned strategy to be put into action in the event of a hostile takeover bid by a black knight.

blind trust /blaɪnd trʌst/ (blind trusts)

INVESTMENT

NOUN A **blind trust** is a financial arrangement in which someone's investments are managed without the person knowing where the money is invested.

○ When a person places securities in a blind trust, by definition he or she does not make the decisions to purchase or sell securities in that account.

○ A politician may be required to place his assets in a blind trust so that his votes are not influenced by his trust's portfolio holdings.

blue-chip /blu tʃɪp/

INVESTMENT: STOCKS

ADJECTIVE A **blue-chip** stock is a stock that has a long stable history of earnings.

○ Analysts say investors should start looking outside the safe haven of blue-chip gold stocks.

○ Certain investors favor small-capitalization stocks, while others prefer large blue-chip stocks.

board of di|rec|tors /bɔrd əv dɪrɛktərz/ (boards of directors)

CORPORATE

NOUN A company's **board of directors** is the group of people elected by the company's shareholders to manage the company.

○ The board of directors has approved the decision unanimously.

○ *The board of directors has not yet decided whether a sale of the company is in the best interest of the company's shareholders and other constituencies.*

---

bolt-on /bəʊlt ɒn/

CORPORATE

ADJECTIVE **Bolt-on** buys are purchases of other companies that a company makes in order to add them to its existing business.

○ *He said the company would make further bolt-on acquisitions in the US.*

○ *Globally, the company aims to close several small bolt-on acquisitions a year, including financial advisory firms, mid-sized private banks, and product specialists.*

---

bond /bɒnd/ (bonds)

INVESTMENT

NOUN A **bond** is a certificate issued to investors when a government or company borrows money from them.

○ *The new credit, which the country will raise through issuing bonds to participating bank creditors, could total as much as $1.2 billion.*

○ *Bond prices strengthened yesterday as investors began to suspect that the Federal Reserve has once again eased credit policy.*

---

bond|hold|er /bɒnd həʊldər/ (bondholders)

INVESTMENT

NOUN A **bondholder** is a person who owns one or more investment bonds.

○ *These covenants provide bondholders with protection in case of credit-damaging events such as a takeover, a leveraged buyout, or a restructuring.*

○ *A bondholder receives his principal and a final interest payment upon a bond's maturity.*

---

bo|nus /bəʊnəs/ (bonuses)

GENERAL

NOUN A **bonus** is an extra amount of money that is paid to shareholders out of profits, or that is given to employees.

B

○ *Each member of staff received a $100 bonus.*

○ *Savings holders may receive a cash bonus of as much as 75 cents a share.*

---

bo|nus is|sue /bounəs ɪʃu/ (bonus issues)

INVESTMENT: STOCKS

NOUN A **bonus issue** is the distribution of free shares of stock among existing shareholders, based on the number of shares they own.

○ *A bonus issue does not really add to shareholder wealth, but is merely an indicator of potential performance.*

○ *The shareholders have done well for themselves in the last year, garnering a 1:2 bonus issue and a 45 percent dividend.*

---

book val|ue¹ /bʊk vælyu/ (book values)

CORPORATE

NOUN **Book value** is the value of a business asset as shown on the company's account books.

○ *He thinks this will produce a large gain in the company's stated book value for the December quarter.*

○ *The insured value of the airplane was greater than its book value.*

---

book val|ue² /bʊk vælyu/ (book values)

INVESTMENT: STOCKS

NOUN **Book value** is the value of a single share of stock, calculated by dividing the value of the company by the number of shares it has issued.

○ *The buyback price was 38% below the stock's book value.*

○ *They were asked to pay about ten times the book value of the stock.*

---

boom /bum/ (booms)

ECONOMICS

NOUN A financial **boom** is an increase in economic activity with rapid growth and rising prices.

○ *China's economic boom has produced a growing hunger for energy that only foreign supplies can satisfy.*

○ *Investment advisers are predicting a boom in oil stocks because an oil shortage is developing.*

---

boom-bust cy|cle /bʊm bʌst saɪkəl/ (**boom-bust cycles**)

ECONOMICS

NOUN A **boom-bust cycle** is a series of events in which a rapid increase in business activity in the economy is followed by a rapid decrease in business activity.

○ *We must avoid the damaging boom-bust cycles which characterized the last decade.*

○ *There was a boom-bust cycle in the asset markets that preceded the currency crisis, in which stock and land prices soared, and then plunged in all of the affected countries.*

---

boot|strap¹ /bʊtstræp/

CORPORATE

ADJECTIVE A **bootstrap** deal is an offer to purchase a controlling share in a company.

○ *Leveraged buyouts, as bootstrap deals came to be known, began as a kind of aid to the elderly.*

○ *A bootstrap transaction occurs when an investor uses leveraged borrowing against the target company's assets to acquire a controlling interest in a company.*

---

boot|strap² /bʊtstræp/ (**bootstraps, bootstrapped, bootstrapping**)

INVESTMENT: VENTURE CAPITALISM

VERB If a business **bootstraps** itself, or an activity, it achieves success with limited resources.

○ *Each kicked in $15,000 of their own money to bootstrap the project for six months.*

○ *Bootstrapping means avoiding external investors, all the while keeping expenses to a minimum.*

B

bot|tom fish|ing /bɒtəm fɪʃɪŋ/

INVESTMENT

NOUN **Bottom fishing** is when you invest in low-priced securities in the hope of making a profit.

o Bottom fishing is an investment strategy based on finding bargains among low-priced stocks.

o Bond traders attributed the rise in prices yesterday to bottom fishing in the wake of Monday's big sell-off.

bot|tom line /bɒtəm laɪn/

CORPORATE

NOUN The **bottom line** is the total amount of money that a company has made or lost over a particular period of time.

o The Japanese threat was enough to force chief executives to look beyond the next quarter's bottom line.

o He recently launched a start-up fund with a small amount of capital and every penny counts toward a positive bottom line.

break|e|ven /breɪkivən/ (short for **breakeven point**)

CORPORATE

NOUN **Breakeven** is the point at which the money a company makes from the sale of goods or services is equal to the money it has spent, so that there is neither profit nor loss.

o "Terminator 2" finally made $200 million, the breakeven point for the movie.

o They had to become a more efficient, lower-cost operation, which meant downsizing the company just to reduce their breakeven point.

break e|ven /breɪk ivən/ (**breaks even, broke even, broken even, breaking even**)

CORPORATE

VERB If a business or person **breaks even**, they earn as much money as they spend but they do not make a profit or a loss.

o The airline hopes to break even next year and return to profit the following year.

○ *The company, which has never made a profit, has predicted it could break even if it could reach a workload of 150 cases a week.*

---

break-up val|ue /breɪkʌp vælyu/ (break-up values)

INVESTMENT: STOCKS

NOUN **Break-up value** is the value of one share of stock in a company based only on the value of the company's assets.

○ *The ruling price of its share at the stock exchange is grossly under-valued relative to its break-up value.*

○ *Plenty of big, healthy companies are valued well below the break-up value of their assets.*

---

bridge loan /brɪdʒ loʊn/ (bridge loans)

BANKING

NOUN A **bridge loan** is money that a bank lends you for a short time, for example so that you can buy a new house before you have sold the one you already own.

○ *Mexico also will get some new lending, including a new US bridge loan of some $2 billion to tide it over until the other credits are made available.*

○ *The transaction will enable the company to repay the balance of a $1.7 billion bridge loan.*

---

bro|ker /broʊkər/ (brokers)

INVESTMENT: STOCKS

NOUN A **broker** is a commissioned agent who buys and sells securities for investors.

○ *In a statement, the company said it hoped the SEC would identify brokers that the company believes engaged in illegal short selling of its stock.*

○ *Online brokers tend to give most of their time and attention to the large accounts while the smaller accounts often fall to the wayside.*

bro|ker|age ac|count /ˈbroʊkərɪdʒ əˈkaʊnt/ (brokerage accounts)

INVESTMENT: STOCKS

NOUN A **brokerage account** is an account with a broker where an investor can buy and sell and hold securities.

○ The recommendation is that the National Association of Securities Dealers adopt a rule to require all broker-dealers to notify a fund when any of the fund's employees open a brokerage account.

○ To buy and sell securities through a broker-dealer or other financial services firm, you establish an account, generally known as a brokerage account, with that firm.

bub|ble /ˈbʌbəl/ (bubbles)

ECONOMICS

NOUN A **bubble** is a situation in which a type of investment such as housing or stocks has prices driven far above actual value by speculators.

○ Amid fears of a property bubble in China, the agency that oversees state-owned firms ordered 78 of the biggest ones to stop dabbling in the property market.

○ It should be no surprise that, after a bubble, prices fall in some areas, and some prices fall more than others.

bull /bʊl/ (bulls)

INVESTMENT: STOCKS

NOUN A **bull** is a person who buys shares of stock when they expect the price to rise in order to make a profit by selling the shares again after a short time.

○ Undeterred, the bulls predict further gains in the months ahead as investors sniff out unrealized potential.

○ A bull expects the market or markets to go up.

bull mar|ket /bʊl mɑrkɪt/ (**bull markets**)

INVESTMENT: STOCKS

NOUN A **bull market** is when people are buying a lot of shares of stock because they expect the price to increase.

○ *There was a decline in prices after the bull market peaked in April 2000.*

○ *Over the past couple of years, gold and silver have stunned the investing mainstream with the strength and persistence of their ongoing bull market trend.*

burn rate /bɜrn reɪt/ (**burn rates**)

INVESTMENT: VENTURE CAPITALISM

NOUN The **burn rate** of a startup company is a measure of how fast it uses up its capital before becoming profitable.

○ *The startup has halved its monthly burn rate and is inching closer to profitability.*

○ *The burn rate on a monthly and quarterly basis is an indication of how much of the initial equity investment is being used up to cover operating expenses.*

bust /bʌst/ (**busts**)

ECONOMICS

NOUN A **bust** is a decrease in economic activity with declining growth and falling prices.

○ *Finance ministries have cut taxes and boosted public spending, which has prevented the biggest financial bust since the 1930s from triggering an economic catastrophe.*

○ *The bust was induced through the decline of lending standards during the boom and the inevitable bankruptcies that induce contraction of bank credit.*

buy for|ward /baɪ fɔrwərd/ (**buys forward, bought forward, buying forward**)

INVESTMENT: STOCKS

VERB If you **buy forward**, you buy at a future date for a price agreed upon today.

○ *As an alternative to buying forward currency, you could borrow dollars, exchange them for foreign currency, and then lend the foreign currency until it is needed.*

B

○ *Hedging by buying forward sterling for dollars will raise the forward premium on sterling.*

RELATED WORDS
Phrasal verbs

There are several other phrasal verbs that are commonly used in finance.

When a company **buys out** another company, they purchase all of the stock of that company.

If you **close out** an account on which the margin is inadequate or exhausted, you terminate it, usually by selling securities to realize cash.

If you **spin off** a company or subsidiary, you sell a subsidiary part of a company, or make a subsidiary its own separate company by issuing shares in the new company.

---

buy out¹ /baɪ aʊt/ (buys out, bought out, buying out)

CORPORATE

VERB When a company **buys out** another company, they purchase all of the stock of that company.

○ *Her resignation sparked speculation that the company might be sold or bought out, sending its stock soaring.*

○ *When the two chains were bought out in 2011, their new parent redirected them into an ambitious, new expansion program.*

---

buy out² /baɪ aʊt/ (buys out, bought out, buying out)

INVESTMENT: STOCKS

VERB If you **buy out** someone, you buy their share of a company or piece of property that you previously owned together.

○ *The bank had to pay to buy out most of the 200 former partners.*

○ *He bought out his brother for $17 million to become the majority shareholder.*

Cc

call /kɔl/ (calls)

INVESTMENT: STOCKS

NOUN A **call** is the right to buy something like a stock or commodity at a certain price.

- You can make money if you buy a call on a stock that goes up in price.
- Zynga call options went up 44 percent in price after Facebook's IPO was announced.

cap|i|tal /kæpɪtəl/

GENERAL

NOUN **Capital** is money that you use to start a business.

- They provide capital for small businesses.
- The value of invested capital is equal to the value of the operating business enterprise.

> **WORD FAMILY**
>
> **capital** NOUN ○ The injection of capital strengthened the company greatly.
>
> **capitalize** VERB ○ These companies were able to lend money to one another and thus capitalize each other.
>
> **capitalization** NOUN ○ The company is now worth less than a fifth of its current stock market capitalization.

C

cap|i|tal ac|count /kæpɪtᵊl əkaʊnt/ (**capital accounts**)

CORPORATE

NOUN A **capital account** is a financial statement showing the net value of a company.

○ *The proprietor's capital account now has a net credit balance of $10,550.*

○ *The capital account is the equity account that shows a sole proprietor's or partner's investment in the business.*

cap|i|tal em|ployed /kæpɪtᵊl ɪmplɔɪd/

CORPORATE

NOUN **Capital employed** is the value of a company's assets minus its liabilities, and represents the investment required to enable the company to operate.

○ *Our marketing business continues to make less than acceptable returns on capital employed.*

○ *Productivity is the amount of output per unit of input, such as the quantity of a product produced per hour of capital employed.*

cap|i|tal ex|pend|i|ture /kæpɪtᵊl ɪkspɛndɪtʃər/

CORPORATE

NOUN In accounting, **capital expenditure** is money that is spent on buying or improving fixed assets.

○ *He plans to cope with the fall in sales by drastically reducing capital expenditure and cutting staff.*

○ *The supermarket chain reduced its capital expenditure from $18 billion to $14 billion.*

cap|i|tal gains /kæpɪtᵊl geɪnz/

INVESTMENT

NOUN **Capital gains** are the profits that you make when you buy a financial asset and then sell it again at a higher price.

○ *Higher capital gains and investment income are offset by increased reserves.*

○ *If the undertaking was owned for less than 36 months, the company will be taxed for short-term capital gains.*

cap|i|tal|i|za|tion /kæpɪtˀlɪzeɪʃˀn/
`GENERAL`

NOUN A **capitalization** is the sum of the total share capital issued by a company.

○ *The company's market capitalization has fallen from $650 million to less than $60 million.*

○ *The firm ended the year with debt equal to 40 percent of total capitalization.*

cap|i|tal|ize /kæpɪtˀlaɪz/ (**capitalizes, capitalized, capitalizing**)
`GENERAL`

VERB If you **capitalize** a business enterprise, you obtain money from somewhere to start or run your business.

○ *We can capitalize the business by borrowing money, looking for private investment, or issuing stock.*

○ *We have found an investor who will capitalize the new bank with about $15 million.*

cap|i|tal lease /kæpɪtˀl liːs/ (**capital leases**)
`GENERAL`

NOUN A **capital lease** is a lease that is treated as the purchase of the asset that is being leased.

○ *A capital lease is thus more like a purchase or sale on installment than a rental.*

○ *Under accounting rules, a capital lease is treated like a purchase.*

cap|i|tal loss /kæpɪtˀl lɔs/ (**capital losses**)
`INVESTMENT`

NOUN A **capital loss** is a loss on investment property.

○ *The fund receives additional income, in the form of a premium, which may offset any capital loss or decline in market value of the security.*

○ *Capital losses can be used to offset capital gains for tax savings.*

C

cap|i|tal stock /ˈkæpɪtᵊl stɒk/

INVESTMENT: STOCKS

NOUN A company's **capital stock** is the money that stockholders invest in order to start or expand the business.

○ *The bank has a capital stock of almost 100 million dollars.*

○ *R&D spending is not shown as capital in their accounts, so that their capital stock is really higher than it appears.*

cash flow /ˈkæʃ floʊ/ (**cash flows**)

GENERAL

NOUN The **cash flow** of a business is the movement of money into and out of it.

○ *The company ran into cash flow problems and faced liquidation.*

○ *Instead of massive investment, they have to finance growth from cash flow, which makes them concentrate on profits.*

cash|ier's check /kæˈʃɪərz tʃɛk/ (**cashier's checks**)

BANKING

NOUN A **cashier's check** is a check that is issued by paying the money to the bank that issues the check, so that the money is guaranteed.

○ *A cashier's check is drawn directly on a customer's account, making the bank the primary obligor, and assuring firms that the amount will be paid.*

○ *Consumers requiring a cashier's check must pay the amount of the check to the bank.*

cash-in-lieu /ˈkæʃ ɪn lu/

INVESTMENT: STOCKS

NOUN **Cash-in-lieu** is payment of cash instead of stock when a stock splits or changes and the shareholder only owns a partial share.

○ *Shareholders must complete and return the form with the securities in order to receive cash-in-lieu payment or exchanged securities.*

○ *Whole shares were issued, and partial shares were paid cash-in-lieu of shares.*

C cor|po|ra|tion /sī kɔrpəreɪʃⁿn/ (**C corporations**)

CORPORATE

NOUN A **C corporation** is a type of corporation that is taxed on its income.

○ *As a C corporation, we have to pay taxes of 39 percent on the portion of our annual earnings between $100,000 and $335,000.*

○ *When a tax return is filed for a C corporation, the corporation pays taxes on the net profit of the business.*

C|D /sī dī/ (short for **certificate of deposit**)

BANKING

ABBREVIATION A **CD** is a savings certificate that is issued by a bank and on which interest is paid.

○ *A CD has a maturity date and a specified interest rate, and can be issued in any denomination.*

○ *The average six-month CD added 0.06 points to 8.78 percent.*

C|D|O /sī di oʊ/ (short for **collateralized debt obligation**)

MORTGAGE

ABBREVIATION A **CDO** is a type of derivative financial investment based on interest-bearing debt such as credit card debt, auto loans, bonds, or mortgage loans.

○ *If cash collected by the CDO is insufficient to pay all of its investors, those in the lower layers suffer losses first.*

○ *CDOs backed by subprime mortgages were a major contributor to the financial crisis.*

cer|ti|fied check (BRIT **certified cheque**) /sɜrtɪfaɪd tʃɛk/ (**certified checks**)

BANKING

NOUN A **certified check** is a check that the issuing bank has guaranteed, saying that there is enough money in the account to pay it.

○ *A certified check is a check issued by a bank, payable to a designated payee, in exchange for cash.*

○ *A certified check legally becomes an obligation of the bank, and the funds to cover it are immediately withdrawn from the depositor's account.*

cer|ti|fied pub|lic ac|count|ant (ABBR **CPA**) /sɜrtɪfaɪd pʌblɪk əkaʊntənt/ (**certified public accountants**)

GENERAL

NOUN A **certified public accountant** is someone who has received a certificate stating that they are qualified to work as an accountant within a particular state of the US.

○ *An independent auditor is a certified public accountant operating outside the company who can provide an accountant's opinion.*

○ *The certified public accountant's report shall state that the audit was made in accordance with US Generally Accepted Auditing Standards.*

check|ing ac|count (in BRIT use **current account**) /tʃɛkɪŋ əkaʊnt/ (**checking accounts**)

BANKING

NOUN A **checking account** is a bank account that you can take money out of by writing a check.

○ *Do not mix business and personal finances by using the same checking account for your home and business.*

○ *He has his checking account at the Commonwealth Bank.*

CHIPS /tʃɪps/ (short for **Clearing House Interbank Payments System**)

BANKING

ABBREVIATION **CHIPS** is a system for transferring funds that makes large value payments in US dollars between major banks.

○ *CHIPS is a computerized mechanism in which banks hold US dollar accounts to pay each other when buying or selling foreign exchange.*

○ *CHIPS records the information received from the member banks.*

---

clear|ing /klɪərɪŋ/

`BANKING`

NOUN **Clearing** is the time that is taken between starting a transaction and finishing it.

○ *The two parties are responsible for arranging the clearing and settlement of any transactions that result from the contract.*

○ *Check clearing can take two to five days.*

---

clear|ing house /klɪərɪŋ haʊs/ (**clearing houses**)

`INVESTMENT: STOCKS`

NOUN A **clearing house** is a financial institution that is an intermediary between two trading firms for securities transactions.

○ *Employees have the right to trade stock among themselves, and the company will establish an internal clearing house for these transactions.*

○ *Fedwire is a major US securities clearing house.*

---

closed-end fund (ABBR **CEF**) /kloʊzd ɛnd fʌnd/
(**closed-end funds**)

`INVESTMENT`

NOUN A **closed-end fund** is an investment with a limited number of shares that does not allow new investors.

○ *Mutual funds can be structured as a closed-end fund, in which a fixed number of nonredeemable shares are sold at an initial offering and then traded in the over-the-counter market like a common stock.*

○ *The market price of a closed-end fund fluctuates in response to investor demand as well as changes in the values of its holdings or its net asset value.*

C

closed-end loan /klouzd ɛnd loʊn/ (**closed-end loans**)

BANKING: CREDIT

NOUN A **closed-end loan** is a loan such as an auto loan, with fixed terms, and where the money is lent all at once and paid back by a particular date.

○ *Closed-end loans, which include installment and student loans and automobile leases, are generally charged off in full no later than when the loan becomes 20 days past due.*

○ *With a closed-end loan, the borrower cannot alter the number and amount of installments, the maturity date, or the credit terms.*

▶ **SYNONYM:**
  installment loan

close out /klouz aʊt/ (**closes out, closed out, closing out**)

INVESTMENT: STOCKS

VERB If you **close out** an account on which the margin is inadequate or exhausted, you terminate it, usually by selling securities to realize cash.

○ *The debit to sales revenue and the credit to expenses close out these accounts.*

○ *He would also close out or set to zero all the revenue and expense accounts for the year in preparation for recording the next year's activity in the following entry.*

C|O|D /si ou di/ (short for **cash on delivery**)

GENERAL

ABBREVIATION **COD** is used to describe payment terms by which cash is paid when goods or services are delivered.

○ *If you are supplying goods to a wide variety of irregular customers, you may require COD.*

○ *Customers quickly get used to the idea of ordering products on the Net, paying with their credit cards or through COD, and having the products delivered to their doorsteps.*

col|lat|er|al /kəlǽtərəl/

BANKING: CREDIT

NOUN **Collateral** is money or property that is used as a guarantee that someone will repay a loan.

○ *Many people use personal assets as collateral for small business loans.*

○ *There is collateral available to be sold if the loans default.*

---

com|mer|cial bank /kəmɜ́rʃ⁹l bǽŋk/ (**commercial banks**)

BANKING

NOUN A **commercial bank** is a bank that takes deposits from and makes loans to individuals and companies.

○ *A commercial bank is a financial institution open to the public for such common transactions as accepting deposits and lending money.*

○ *Britain raised commercial bank lending rates to 15 percent in an effort to defend the pound from further declines.*

---

com|mer|cial pa|per /kəmɜ́rʃ⁹l péɪpər/ (**commercial papers**)

INVESTMENT

NOUN **Commercial paper** refers to short term loans issued by large corporations without any security.

○ *Since it is not backed by collateral, only firms with excellent credit ratings from a recognized rating agency will be able to sell their commercial paper at a reasonable price.*

○ *The most common maturity range of commercial paper is 30 to 50 days or less.*

---

com|mis|sion /kəmɪ́ʃ⁹n/

INVESTMENT: STOCKS

NOUN **Commission** is payment to a broker of part of the profits from a sale.

○ *Travel agents charge 1 percent commission on tickets.*

○ *The salespeople work on commission only.*

C

com|mod|i|ty /kəmɒdɪti/ (commodities)

INVESTMENT

NOUN A **commodity** is an item that is traded on the market, such as wheat, gold, silver, oil, coffee, or sugar.

○ The corporation provided $150 million to finance the exports of various commodities and food goods including cotton and tobacco.

○ Commodities widely traded on exchanges around the world are agricultural products and raw materials such as oil and copper.

> **TALKING ABOUT COMMODITIES**
>
> People **trade** commodities when they buy and sell them. If they buy commodities from another country, they **import** them, and if they sell them to another country, they **export** them.

com|mon stock /kɒmən stɒk/

INVESTMENT: STOCKS

NOUN **Common stock** is the shares in a company that are owned by people who have a right to vote at company meetings and to receive part of the company's profits after the holders of preferred stock have been paid.

○ The company priced its offering of 2.7 million shares of common stock at 20 cents a share.

○ The banking concern said that under the plan, shareholders will exchange their common stock for an equal number of shares in the new holding company.

com|pound in|ter|est /kɒmpaʊnd ɪntrɪst/

GENERAL

NOUN **Compound interest** is interest that is paid both on an original sum of money and on interest that has already been paid on that sum.

○ When money is invested at compound interest, each interest payment is reinvested to earn more interest in subsequent periods.

○ We compute compound interest on principal and on any interest earned that has not been paid or withdrawn.

con|tan|go /kəntæŋgoʊ/

INVESTMENT

NOUN **Contango** is a situation in which the price of a forward or futures contract is trading above the expected spot price when the contract matures.

○ Contango is the term applied when the contract price promised in a futures market upon delivery of an item is higher the more distant in time the delivery will occur.

○ A contango is observed when the futures price is higher than the spot or cash price.

> **WORD ORIGINS**
>
> This word originated in 19th century England, and is believed to be a corruption of the word "continue" or "contingent."

con|ven|tion|al mort|gage /kənvɛnʃənəl mɔrgɪdʒ/
(conventional mortgages)

MORTGAGE

NOUN A **conventional mortgage** is a fixed rate mortgage with a standard term of 15, 20, or 30 years.

○ At 10 percent interest, $250 a month will support a 30-year conventional mortgage worth nearly $28,500.

○ The average rate on a 30-year conventional mortgage in New York state was 10.04 percent.

> **RELATED WORDS**
> **Mortgages**
>
> An **ARM** is a type of mortgage where the interest rate may change according to changes in other rates and a **balloon mortgage** is a mortgage in which you make small payments over a period of time and repay the balance in one large final payment.
>
> A **HELOC** is an additional loan secured by a residence as well as the original mortgage, whereas a **reverse mortgage** is a mortgage on a paid-off property that provides money to an older retired person, to be paid back when the property is sold or when the person dies.

C

con|vert|i|ble /kənvɜrtɪbəl/

INVESTMENT

ADJECTIVE **Convertible** stock or bonds are preferred stock or bonds that can be converted into common stock.

○ *A convertible bond is a bond with an option, allowing the bondholder to exchange the bond for a specified number of shares of common stock in a firm.*

○ *Convertible bonds give the investor the option to change them into stock rather than receiving a cash redemption.*

con|vert|i|ble cur|ren|cy /kənvɜrtɪbəl kɜrənsi/
(convertible currencies)

FOREIGN EXCHANGE

NOUN A **convertible currency** is a currency that can be bought and sold on the open market for other currencies.

○ *Bonds can be denominated in any freely convertible currency.*

○ *A gold-backed ruble would be seen as an honest money at home and would immediately trade as a convertible currency internationally.*

cor|po|rate ven|tur|ing /kɔrpərɪt vɛntʃərɪŋ/

INVESTMENT: VENTURE CAPITALISM

NOUN **Corporate venturing** is when one company provides venture capital for another company as part of a plan to acquire that company.

○ *Corporate venturing can have an external focus – investing in strategically related technology startups, for example – or an internal focus.*

○ *Perhaps the most significant potential source of equity finance in high-tech sectors such as pharmaceuticals and software may be corporate venturing.*

cor|po|ra|tion /kɔrpəreɪʃən/ (corporations)

CORPORATE

NOUN A **corporation** is a large business or company.

○ *The interests of management and shareholders often conflict, particularly when a corporation is subject to a possible takeover attempt.*

○ *The nation's largest corporations aren't directly affected by prime rate changes because many can borrow at rates well below the prime.*

cor|re|spond|ent bank /kɔ̠rɪspɒndənt bæŋk/
(**correspondent banks**)

BANKING

NOUN A **correspondent bank** is a bank that provides services such as accepting deposits for another bank.

○ *Agreements to reciprocate are usual, specifying which services a bank will perform for a correspondent bank.*

○ *Each money center bank has hundreds of correspondent banks that call their money desk each morning to ask what the prime rate is for the day.*

cost of cap|i|tal /kɔst əv kæpɪtᵊl/

INVESTMENT

NOUN The **cost of capital** is how much it costs to borrow money with interest or issue securities to raise money.

○ *It is the cost of capital that influences the behavior of savers and investors and that is relevant for judging the efficiency of the tax system.*

○ *The manager must determine whether the net present value of the investment to the enterprise is positive using the marginal cost of capital that is associated with the particular area of business.*

coun|ter|of|fer /kaʊntərɔfər/ (**counteroffers**)

GENERAL

NOUN A **counteroffer** is a reply to an original offer suggesting a change of terms.

○ *Negotiation is a process of making offers and counteroffers, with the aim of finding an acceptable agreement.*

○ *The company rejected the investor's counteroffer.*

cou|pon rate /kupɒn reɪt/ (**coupon rates**)

INVESTMENT

NOUN The **coupon rate** is the interest rate on a bond calculated on the number of coupons per year.

C

○ A tax-exempt municipal bond has a higher after-tax yield than a corporate bond with the same coupon rate.

○ This five-year paper has a coupon rate of 6 percent.

---

cov|er /kʌvər/ (covers, covered, covering)
GENERAL

VERB If you **cover** a liability, you have enough money to pay it.

○ Direct overheads are the part of overhead costs devoted to the manufacturing sector of a firm to cover expenses such as rent and utilities.

○ Some of the company's large stock of assets are likely to be sold to cover the debts.

▶ **COLLOCATIONS:**
cover a debt
cover expenses

---

cred|it bu|reau /krɛdɪt byʊəroʊ/ (credit bureaus)
BANKING: CREDIT

NOUN A **credit bureau** is a company that provides information to banks and other lenders about whether borrowers will be able to pay back their loans.

○ The credit bureau issues a report that shows a loan applicant's history of payments made on previous debts.

○ You can get information on the experience that other firms have had with your customer by contacting a credit bureau.

---

cred|it rat|ing /krɛdɪt reɪtɪŋ/ (credit ratings)
BANKING: CREDIT

NOUN A **credit rating** is a judgement about whether a borrower will be able to pay back a loan, based on their past history.

○ The better your credit rating is, the better financing alternatives will be available for you.

○ Before such an agreement is concluded, the counterparty's credit rating must be examined to reassure the project of the party's ability to meet its obligations.

cred|it risk /krɛdɪt rɪsk/ (**credit risks**)

BANKING: CREDIT

NOUN A **credit risk** is the risk that money that has been lent will not be repaid.

○ *Companies carry credit risk when, for example, they do not demand upfront cash payment for products or services.*

○ *We seek to be the preferred supplier to high-volume, high-margin customers with the lowest credit risk.*

cred|it score /krɛdɪt skɔr/ (**credit scores**)

BANKING: CREDIT

NOUN A borrower's **credit score** is a number calculated by a credit bureau to express how likely they are to be able to pay back their loans.

○ *There was a time when a bad credit score would hold you from receiving any kind of credit or loans, but not anymore.*

○ *Firms that handle a large volume of credit information often use a formal system for combining the various sources into an overall credit score.*

cred|it swap /krɛdɪt swɒp/ (**credit swaps**)

INVESTMENT

NOUN A **credit swap** is a kind of insurance against credit risk where a third party agrees to pay a lender if the loan defaults, in exchange for receiving payments from the lender.

○ *A credit swap is an alternative method of obtaining debt capital for a foreign subsidiary without sending funds abroad.*

○ *The buyer of a credit swap will be paid by the seller if the security defaults.*

▶ **SYNONYM:**
credit default swap

cred|it un|ion /krɛdɪt yunyən/ (**credit unions**)

BANKING

NOUN A **credit union** is a not-for-profit financial institution that is owned cooperatively by the people who keep their money there.

○ Sales by the credit union of any of the stock purchased by one of its members would occur only in satisfaction of a delinquent loan balance.

○ A credit union will pay a dividend to represent interest on a saver's deposit.

---

cross rate /krɒs reɪt/ (cross rates)

FOREIGN EXCHANGE

NOUN A **cross rate** is an exchange rate of two currencies expressed in a third different currency, such as the exchange rate between the euro and the yuan expressed in yen.

○ The dollar's jump was linked initially to a temporary reversal on the busy yen-mark cross rate that prompted a quick retreat out of the German currency and indirectly boosted the dollar.

○ The cross rate refers to the exchange rate between two currencies, each of which has an exchange rate quote against a common currency.

C|S|O /si ɛs oʊ/ (short for **common stock outstanding, common shares outstanding**)

INVESTMENT: STOCKS

ABBREVIATION CSO is the amount of shares of common stock that have been issued and are owned by investors.

○ Earnings per share can be calculated as net income divided by average CSO.

○ CSO is the amount of shares that have been issued minus treasury stock repurchased.

---

cum div|i|dend /kʊm dɪvɪdɛnd/

INVESTMENT: STOCKS

ADJECTIVE Investors who buy a share **cum dividend** are entitled to receive a recently issued dividend. "Cum" is Latin, meaning "with."

○ Stocks are usually cum dividend for trades made on or before the fifth trading day preceding the record date.

○ At the time of acquisition the company has announced that it is to make a distribution of 1,500 shares cum dividend.

cu|mu|la|tive /kyūmyələtɪv/

INVESTMENT: STOCKS

ADJECTIVE **Cumulative** dividends or earnings are added on from period to period.

○ *Analysts estimate that third-quarter earnings for the industry will increase as much as 19 percent from the year-earlier period. If so, their cumulative earnings could hit $4.12 billion.*

○ *The Fund provided a six-month cumulative return of 3.26 percent.*

cur|rent yield /kɜrənt yīld/ (**current yields**)

INVESTMENT

NOUN The **current yield** of a bond is the interest payment divided by the current price of the bond.

○ *Because a security's price may rise or fall after issuance, its current yield may be higher or lower than its coupon.*

○ *The longer the bond's maturity and the closer the bond's market value is to its par value, the better the current yield is as a predictor of the bond's yield to maturity.*

CU|SIP num|ber /kyūsɪp nʌmbər/ (short for **Committee on Uniform Securities Indentification Procedures number**) (**CUSIP numbers**)

INVESTMENT

NOUN A **CUSIP number** is a number that identifies an individual security like a stock or a bond.

○ *A quarterly transaction report should include the CUSIP number for each security for which a transaction occurred and the date that the report was submitted.*

○ *A CUSIP number is the universal security identification for each type of security.*

cus|to|di|an bank /kʌstōudiən bæŋk/ (**custodian banks**)

BANKING

NOUN A **custodian bank** is a bank that holds customer assets in safety.

○ The sponsor of these certificates or receipts typically purchases and deposits the securities in an irrevocable trust or custodial account with a custodian bank.

○ An amount of cash must be deposited with the broker as initial margin as a good faith deposit, and is generally maintained in a segregated account at the custodian bank.

cus|toms du|ty /kʌstəmz duti/

TAX

NOUN **Customs duty** is a tax that people pay for importing and exporting goods.

○ Foreign investors can now import and export goods without paying customs duties.

○ Customs duty on some capital goods used by the telecoms sector has come down from 25 percent to 15 percent.

cut|off time (or **cut-off time**) /kʌtɔf taɪm/ (**cutoff times**)

BANKING

NOUN The **cutoff time** is the time at which a bank stops crediting same-day deposits.

○ Deposits after the cutoff time are credited the next banking day.

○ Bank cutoff times determine when a transaction is official, so you should know your institution's rules.

Dd

deal|er /ˈdiːlər/ (dealers)

INVESTMENT

NOUN A **dealer** is a broker who can hold a position in the securities they sell.

○ A dealer trading shares charges a percentage of the dollar amount of the trade.

○ Each dealer has a password that allows access to updated stock information.

de|ben|ture /dɪˈbɛntʃər/ (debentures)

INVESTMENT

NOUN A **debenture** is an unsecured corporate bond.

○ The subsidiary issues debentures overseas and invests the proceeds in foreign operations.

○ Unlike a mortgage bond, a debenture is generally not secured by a mortgage or lien on any specific property.

debt cov|e|nant /dɛt ˈkʌvənənt/ (debt covenants)

BANKING: CREDIT

NOUN A **debt covenant** is a number of restrictions that a borrower agrees to that are set by the lending institution.

○ The credit quality of a loan may be affected by a borrower's failure to comply with debt covenant terms.

○ A positive debt covenant is one in which the borrower is considered to be in default on all debts if they are in default on any debt to any lender.

▶ **SYNONYM:**
banking covenant

debt re|lief /dɛt rɪlif/

BANKING: CREDIT

NOUN **Debt relief** is a situation in which part of a debt is written off or the amount owed is reduced.

○ The debt accord would require major bank creditors to contribute to a $1.2 billion loan or offer the country some debt relief.

○ The IMF will finance debt relief for poor countries.

debt re|struc|tur|ing /dɛt ristrʌktʃərɪŋ/

CORPORATE

NOUN **Debt restructuring** is a method of organizing a company's debts in a different way in order to make the company more likely to be able to pay them.

○ The firm finally announced a debt restructuring agreement with its banks.

○ Debt restructuring is usually less expensive and a preferable alternative to bankruptcy.

debt swap /dɛt swɒp/ (**debt swaps**)

INVESTMENT

NOUN A **debt swap** is a legal agreement where two people or companies exchange their debts, often where one has a fixed interest rate and one does not.

○ The company took steps to withdraw its proposed debt swap for $500 million in high-interest notes.

○ The president wants to force through a unilateral debt swap and prevent the Fund from pushing for better terms for creditors.

debt-to-eq|ui|ty ra|ti|o /dɛt tu ɛkwɪti reɪʃoʊ/ (**debt-to-equity ratios**)

CORPORATE: ACCOUNTING

NOUN A company's **debt-to-equity ratio** is a measure of leverage that is calculated by dividing total liabilities by shareholders' equity.

○ The debt-to-equity ratio reveals the proportion of debt and equity a company is using to finance its business.

○ *The debt-to-equity ratio indicates how the firm finances its operations with debt relative to the book value of its shareholders' equity.*

de|fault¹ /dɪfɔlt/ (defaults)

GENERAL

NOUN A **default** is a failure to pay money that is owed.

○ *Investors should ask whether it makes sense to insure against a default on Treasury bonds.*

○ *A good rating is not an iron-clad guarantee against a default, but, at least it provides an objective assessment of the company's repayment capacity.*

de|fault² /dɪfɔlt/ (defaults, defaulted, defaulting)

GENERAL

VERB If a person or organization **defaults on** a payment, they fail to pay an amount they owe.

○ *Purchasers of bonds need to know whether a corporation is likely to default on its bonds.*

○ *The credit card business is down, and more borrowers are defaulting on loans.*

de|mand curve /dɪmænd kɜrv/ (demand curves)

ECONOMICS

NOUN A **demand curve** is a graph showing the price of an item and the amount consumers want to buy.

○ *A change in quantity demanded is a result of a change in the price of the goods, and is reflected in a movement from one point to another on a given demand curve.*

○ *It is generally assumed that the demand curve is downward sloping: as prices go up, demand goes down.*

de|mand note /dɪmænd noʊt/ (demand notes)

BANKING: CREDIT

NOUN A **demand note** is a loan where the lender can demand repayment at any time.

○ *A demand note allows the noteholder (lender) to call the note due at any time.*

○ *Courts have restricted the circumstances under which a bank could enforce a demand for repayment under a demand note.*

---

de|mu|tu|al|i|za|tion /dimyutʃuəlızeɪʃ°n/

CORPORATE

NOUN Demutualization is a situation in which a mutually owned company such as an insurance company changes into a public company that issues stock.

○ *The process of converting an exchange from a mutual ownership organization to a stock ownership organization is called demutualization.*

○ *The major reason for the demutualization of advance-premium mutual life insurers is the need for additional capital to remain competitive.*

> **WORD BUILDER**
> **de-** = opposite
>
> The prefix **de-** is often used in words connected with changing something to an opposite state: **demutualization**, **depreciation**, **devaluation**, **devalue**.

---

de|pre|ci|a|tion /dɪpriʃieɪʃən/

GENERAL

NOUN Depreciation is the decrease in the exchange value of one currency against another currency.

○ *A bear is a trader who goes short or advocates going short in the expectation of a depreciation of a currency.*

○ *The Australian dollar has rebounded from a tumble it took in mid-July, when a British brokerage firm predicted a sharp depreciation in the currency.*

---

de|riv|a|tive /dɪrɪvətɪv/ (**derivatives**)

INVESTMENT

NOUN A **derivative** is an investment that depends on the value of something else.

○ *Interest rate derivatives are used in structured finance transactions to control interest rate risk with respect to changes in the level of interest rates.*

○ Typically, derivatives are significantly more volatile than the underlying securities on which they are based.

---

de|val|u|a|tion /dɪvælyueɪʃᵊn/

FOREIGN EXCHANGE

NOUN **Devaluation** is a deliberate decrease in the exchange value of a currency against another currency that is made by a government.

○ It will lead to devaluation of a number of currencies.

○ This sector has been badly hit, particularly since the devaluation of South East Asian currencies.

---

de|val|ue /dɪvælyu/ (**devalues, devalued, devaluing**)

FOREIGN EXCHANGE

VERB If a government **devalues** the currency of a country, it reduces its value in relation to other currencies.

○ India has devalued the rupee by about eleven percent.

○ Spiraling debt and printing money is what will destroy the US economy and devalue the dollar.

---

di|lu|tion /daɪluʃᵊn/

INVESTMENT: STOCKS

NOUN **Dilution** is a situation in which more common stock is issued, making each individual share worth less than it was before.

○ The increase in dilution was caused by the increase in stock price since the beginning of the year.

○ Dilution is a reduction in the percentage ownership of a given shareholder in a company caused by the issuance of new shares.

---

di|min|ish|ing re|turns /dɪmɪnɪʃɪŋ rɪtɜrnz/

ECONOMICS

NOUN **Diminishing returns** is a situation in which production, profits, or benefits increase less and less as more money is spent or more effort is made.

○ *Volume growth need not necessarily be accompanied by diminishing returns, although the risk is quite real.*

○ *Adding more workers without increasing the number of machines will lead to diminishing returns.*

---

di|rect deb|it /dɪrɛkt dɛbɪt/ (**direct debits**)

BANKING

NOUN A **direct debit** is an electronic withdrawal of funds from a checking account for payment.

○ *More people are being encouraged to pay their bills automatically by standing order or direct debit.*

○ *You can purchase books online with a credit card or by direct debit.*

---

di|rect de|pos|it /dɪrɛkt dɪpɒzɪt/ (**direct deposits**)

BANKING

NOUN A **direct deposit** is money transferred directly into a bank account.

○ *Direct deposit is commonly used for payroll in the US without a paper paycheck being issued.*

○ *Security recipients receive their payments through direct deposit.*

---

di|rect pub|lic of|fer|ing (ABBR **DPO**) /dɪrɛkt pʌblɪk ɔfərɪŋ/ (**direct public offerings**)

INVESTMENT: VENTURE CAPITALISM

NOUN A **direct public offering** is stock offered directly for sale to investors by a company without the use of underwriters or brokers.

○ *He recruited investors for his company in a direct public offering done entirely over the Internet.*

○ *Direct public offerings are an alternative to underwritten public offerings.*

---

dis|count|ed cash flow (ABBR **DCF**) /dɪskaʊntɪd kæʃ floʊ/

ECONOMICS

NOUN **Discounted cash flow** is a way of appraising an investment that takes into account the different values of future returns according to when they will be received.

○ The purpose of discounted cash flow is to estimate market value, or to estimate what investors would pay for a stock or business.

○ Discounted cash flow is a cash flow associated with economic projects that are adjusted to allow for the timing of the cash flow and the potential interest on the funds involved.

---

dis|count rate /dɪskaʊnt reɪt/ (discount rates)

BANKING

NOUN The **discount rate** is the Federal Reserve rate for short term loans to commercial banks.

○ On all loans, national banks may charge 1.0 percent more than the discount rate on 90-day commercial paper.

○ Wednesday's rise in the discount rate failed to curb the dollar's rise against the yen.

---

dis|cre|tion|ar|y trust /dɪskrɛʃənɛri trʌst/ (discretionary trusts)

INVESTMENT

NOUN A **discretionary trust** is a trust where the amounts paid to the people named are not fixed but are decided by the trustees.

○ The management of a discretionary trust decides on the best way to use the assets without restriction to a specific type of security.

○ A discretionary trust gives the trustee discretion to pay out any trust income deemed desirable to a deceased's surviving spouse during his or her lifetime.

---

dis|in|vest[1] /dɪsɪnvɛst/ (disinvests, disinvested, disinvesting)

INVESTMENT

VERB To **disinvest in** a company is to remove investment from it.

○ They use information from the financial statements in order to determine whether or not they are going to invest or disinvest in a company.

○ If we find good buyers for our non-core businesses at the right price, where employee interests are also protected, we would not hesitate to disinvest.

dis|in|vest² /dɪsɪnvɛst/ (disinvests, disinvested, disinvesting)

CORPORATE

VERB To **disinvest** is to reduce the capital stock of an economy or a company.

○ *The area and buildings of the Management Development Center were part of the assets to be disinvested.*

○ *Our current policy is to disinvest, and obsolete machinery will not be replaced.*

dis|tri|bu|tion /dɪstrɪbyuʃ°n/

INVESTMENT: STOCKS

NOUN A **distribution** is an amount that is paid to stockholders or investors.

○ *These funds claim to pay out annual distributions of more than 11 percent.*

○ *From the proceeds, the company said it will declare a distribution of $7.50 a share to its shareholders.*

di|ver|si|fi|ca|tion /dɪvɜrsɪfɪkeɪʃ°n/

INVESTMENT

NOUN **Diversification** is the act of investing in different industries, areas, countries, and types of financial instruments, to reduce the chance that all of the investments will drop in price at the same time.

○ *Diversification involves dividing investment funds among a variety of securities with different risk, reward, and correlation statistics so as to minimize unsystematic risk.*

○ *Through diversification, investors can offset losses on some investments with gains on others.*

di|vest /dɪvɛst/ (divests, divested, divesting)

GENERAL

VERB If you **divest yourself of** an asset, you get rid of it, usually by selling it.

○ *The company divested itself of its oil interests.*

○ *Negotiators agreed to force thrifts to divest themselves of any non-investment grade bonds and direct equity investments within five years.*

div|i|dend /dɪvidɛnd/ (dividends)

INVESTMENT: STOCKS

NOUN A **dividend** is an amount of a company's profits that is paid to people who own shares in the company.

○ *The first quarter dividend has been increased by nearly 4 percent.*

○ *The company's acquisitions will eventually result in higher dividends for shareholders.*

div|i|dend cov|er /dɪvidɛnd kʌvər/

CORPORATE

NOUN A company's **dividend cover** is the number of times that its dividends could be paid out of its annual profits after tax.

○ *With falling profits, analysts worry that the firm's dividend cover is slim.*

○ *Dividend cover provides an indication of the company's present capacity to repeat the most recent dividends.*

dol|lar cost av|er|ag|ing (ABBR DCA) /dɒlər kɔst ævərədʒɪŋ/

INVESTMENT

NOUN **Dollar cost averaging** is the act of investing a set amount in stocks or other securities during each accounting period, so that you buy more when the price is low and less when the price is high.

○ *Thanks to dollar cost averaging, you don't have to worry whether the market is up or down.*

○ *Dollar cost averaging works best with volatile investments, and it is when prices are down that you are really planting the seeds for future profits.*

Ee

earn|ings per share (ABBR **EPS**) /ˈɜrnɪŋz pər ʃɛər/

INVESTMENT: STOCKS

NOUN **Earnings per share** are the amount of net income from shares divided by the total number of shares outstanding.

○ Shareholders will suffer about a 15 percent dilution in earnings per share.

○ They expect about 10 percent growth in earnings per share, indicating share earnings of about $2.64 for the period.

E|BIT|DA /ˈiːbɪtdɑ/ (short for **earnings before interest, tax, depreciation, and amortization**)

CORPORATE

NOUN **EBITDA** is the amount of profit that a person or company receives before interest, taxes, depreciation, and amortization have been deducted.

○ Now, we had an EBITDA profit of 60 million and a net profit of 10 million.

○ The company has managed in three years to boost sales by nearly 400 percent while dramatically increasing both EBITDA and owners' compensation.

E|C|B /ˈi si bi/ (short for **European Central Bank**)

BANKING

ABBREVIATION The **ECB** is the central bank for the countries of the European Union that share the euro currency.

○ The ECB was created to monitor the monetary policy of the countries that converted to the Euro from their local currencies.

○ The clamor for the ECB to cut interest rates is likely to grow louder as the bank's next meeting approaches.

ef|fi|cient fron|tier /ɪfɪʃənt frʌntɪər/ (**efficient frontiers**)

ECONOMICS

NOUN The **efficient frontier** is a method of analyzing a portfolio to discover the combination of assets that will produce the most return for risk.

○ *The efficient frontier represents the set of portfolios that will give you the highest return at each level of risk.*

○ *Implicit in building the efficient frontier is the choice of risky assets.*

E|F|T /i ɛf ti/ (short for **electronic funds transfer**)

BANKING

ABBREVIATION **EFT** is a transfer of funds that is carried out electronically.

○ *EFT systems eliminate the paperwork of purchase orders, invoices, and checks.*

○ *The amount of the investment will be electronically deducted from her account by EFT.*

e|lec|tron|ic check con|ver|sion (BRIT electronic cheque conversion) /ɪlɛktrɒnɪk tʃɛk kənvɜrʒ°n/

BANKING

NOUN **Electronic check conversion** is the act of processing a paper check as an electronic transaction.

○ *With electronic check conversion, you give a payee a check, but the actual payment is processed as an electronic funds transfer.*

○ *A business must notify you before it uses electronic check conversion to process your payment.*

en|dorse /ɪndɔrs/ (**endorses, endorsed, endorsing**)

BANKING

VERB If you **endorse** a check or other financial instrument, you sign it to make it negotiable.

○ *Both parties are required to endorse the back of the bank draft before it is honored by the bank.*

○ *Not one bank teller made her endorse the checks even though she was receiving the funds.*

eq|ui|ty /ˈɛkwɪti/

CORPORATE

NOUN **Equity** is the sum of the assets or investments of a business after liabilities have been subtracted.

○ *To capture their equity, they must either sell or refinance.*

○ *The company is considering raising part of its future capital requirements by selling equity to the public.*

es|cheat /ɪsˈtʃiːt/

BANKING

NOUN **Escheat** is a situation in which the money in a bank account reverts to the government because the account has been inactive for a long time and the account holder cannot be located.

○ *If there is no activity in an account for five years or more, the account may be subject to escheat procedures in which the account's assets revert to the state.*

○ *The assets subject to the laws of escheat include both securities and cash balances in accounts.*

es|crow /ˈɛskrəʊ/

GENERAL

NOUN **Escrow** is money held by an independent third party to facilitate a financial transaction between two other parties.

○ *The remainder of the money will be held in escrow until a judge determines who is entitled to the proceeds.*

○ *A purchaser will deposit a fund into the escrow account and the money won't be released to the seller till a guaranteed delivery is made.*

E|SOP /ˈiːsɒp/ (short for **employee stock option plan**)

INVESTMENT: STOCKS

ABBREVIATION An **ESOP** is a system by which some employees of a company have the right to buy shares in the company at a particular price.

○ *The firm didn't have a very meaningful retirement plan, so an ESOP was set up for the firm's 103 employees.*

○ *Through an ESOP, a certain number of shares is reserved for purchase and issuance to key employees.*

E|T|F /ˌi ti ˈɛf/ (short for **exchange traded fund**)

INVESTMENT

ABBREVIATION An **ETF** is an investment fund that trades like stock on an exchange.

○ *ETFs made it possible for investors to invest in a variety of other instruments like gold and silver just like investing in stocks.*

○ *Because of the limited redeemability of ETF shares, they are not considered to be and may not call themselves mutual funds.*

Eu|ro|dol|lars /ˈyʊəroʊdɒlərz/

FOREIGN EXCHANGE

NOUN **Eurodollars** are deposits in financial institutions that are not in the US that are denominated in US dollars.

○ *The differential between the interest rate on Eurodollars and the rate on domestic deposits narrowed.*

○ *The international banks also make unsecured loans of Eurodollars, with the rates usually tied to LIBOR.*

---

ex|change rate /ɪkstʃˈeɪndʒ reɪt/ (**exchange rates**)

FOREIGN EXCHANGE

NOUN The **exchange rate** of a country's unit of currency is the amount of another country's currency that you get in exchange for it.

○ *The exchange rate was becoming steadily more and more overvalued, which meant that import prices were falling.*

○ *The cost booked at the date of purchase uses the exchange rate at that date.*

TALKING ABOUT EXCHANGE RATES

A **favorable** exchange rate is one that gives you an advantage. If exchange rates are getting worse, they are **falling**, and if they are getting better, they are **rising**.

A **fixed** exchange rate is one that will not change.

ex div|i|dend /ɛks dɪvɪdɛnd/

INVESTMENT: STOCKS

ADJECTIVE If a share is sold **ex dividend**, the recent dividend stays with the seller rather than going to the buyer.

○ Investors who buy a share ex dividend are obliged to return the dividend if they receive it.

○ When a security is sold ex dividend, the dividend remains with the seller.

ex-div|i|dend date /ɛks dɪvɪdɛnd deɪt/ (**ex-dividend dates**)

INVESTMENT: STOCKS

NOUN The **ex-dividend date** is the date after the declaration of a dividend on which the buyer of a stock is not entitled to receive the next dividend payment.

○ After the ex-dividend date, purchasers are no longer entitled to the dividend.

○ It is relatively common for a stock's price to decrease on the ex-dividend date by an amount roughly equal to the dividend paid.

ex|er|cise price /ɛksərsaɪz praɪs/ (**exercise prices**)

INVESTMENT: STOCKS

NOUN The **exercise price** is the price at which the holder of a traded option is allowed to buy or sell a security.

○ Investment bankers advised the company to set the exercise price at a level three times its stock price.

○ Investment bankers advised the company to set the exercise price at a level three times its stock price.

ex|po|sure /ɪkspoʊʒər/

GENERAL

NOUN **Exposure** is the risk that a loss might occur.

○ Financial advice for small businesses can identify and maximize growth opportunities and minimize exposure to foreign currency fluctuations.

○ Hedge funds employ innovative investment strategies to attain relatively high returns while simultaneously reducing exposure to market risk.

Ff

face val|ue /feɪs vælyu/

INVESTMENT: STOCKS

NOUN The **face value** of stock is the amount shown on the certificate, or, for bonds, the maturity value.

○ *The company's bonds have fallen to 28 percent of their face value.*

○ *There is some possibility that the issuer of the securities may not be able to pay back the face value of the securities when they mature.*

fac|tor|ing /fæktərɪŋ/

GENERAL

NOUN **Factoring** is the act of selling the right to collect receivables for a percentage of their value.

○ *The provision of credit by making loans and purchasing accounts receivable at a discount is known as factoring.*

○ *The factoring firm pays a percentage of the invoices immediately, and the remainder when the accounts receivable are actually paid off by the firm's customers.*

fair mar|ket val|ue (ABBR **FMV**) /feər markɪt vælyu/

GENERAL

NOUN The **fair market value** of an asset is what a willing buyer would pay a willing seller for it on the open market.

○ *The board adopted a shareholder rights plan designed to assure holders fair market value in the event of a proposed takeover.*

○ *Investments must be held at fair market value – the price at which they can be sold to a third party in an orderly transaction.*

Fan|nie Mae /fænɪ meɪ/ (short for **Federal National Mortgage Association**)

MORTGAGE

NOUN **Fannie Mae** is an official organization in the US that buys and sells loans in order to provide mortgages to homebuyers.

○ *Fannie Mae purchases residential mortgages and converts them into securities for sale to investors.*

○ *Fannie Mae is one of several government agencies that is permitted to issue debt for sale to the investing public.*

WORD ORIGINS

The nickname **Fannie Mae** derives from the initials of its formal name, the Federal National Mortgage Association.

Similarly, the Federal Home Loan Mortgage Association is known as **Freddie Mac**, the Government National Mortgage Association is **Ginnie Mae**, and the Student Loan Marketing Association is **Sallie Mae**.

F|D|I|C /ɛf di aɪ si/ (short for **Federal Deposit Insurance Corporation**)

BANKING

ABBREVIATION The **FDIC** is a corporation in the US that insures deposits in national banks and financial institutions against bank failure.

○ *The FDIC was created to protect the consumer against bank or savings and loan failure.*

○ *The FDIC will allow borrowers whose loan has not been purchased by another institution the opportunity to find another bank who will take over the loan.*

---

fed|er|al funds rate /fɛdərəl fʌndz reɪt/

BANKING

NOUN The **federal funds rate** is the overnight rate between banks.

○ *As long as foreign banks continue to want US debt, then the international interest rate set by the bond market bypasses the federal funds rate.*

○ *The Federal Reserve has begun to increase the federal funds rate on a consistent basis, and lending rates will undoubtedly increase.*

Fed|er|al Re|serve (ABBR **The Fed**) /fɛdərəl rɪzɜrv/

BANKING

NOUN The **Federal Reserve** is the central bank that issues money in the US.

○ *The Federal Reserve was born in 1913 and was instituted to solve the problem of coordinating the inflation of the currency and the need to bail out banks in trouble.*

○ *Deposit institutions are required by the Federal Reserve to maintain reserves above a minimum requirement.*

Fed|wire /fɛdwaɪər/ (short for **Federal Reserve Wire Network**)

BANKING

NOUN The **Fedwire** is an electronic system for transferring large sums of money and securities between banks.

○ *The primary wire transfer system, known as Fedwire, is run by the Federal Reserve System and is available to all depository institutions.*

○ *Depository institutions transfer large-dollar payments over the Fedwire.*

FI|CO /faɪkoʊ/ (short for **Fair Isaac Corporation**)

BANKING: CREDIT

ABBREVIATION **FICO** is a corporation that issues credit risk scores.

○ *New borrowers will now be required to have a minimum FICO score of 580 to qualify for the 3.5 percent down payment program.*

○ *FICO refers to a person's credit score based on credit history.*

fi|du|ci|ar|y /fɪduʃieri/ (**fiduciaries**)

GENERAL

NOUN A **fiduciary** is someone who is responsible for making monetary decisions for someone else.

○ *A fiduciary will hold assets for another party with the authority and duty to make decisions in the best interests of that other party.*

○ *In general legal terms, a fiduciary is anyone responsible for another party's money or property.*

F

fi|nance charge /faɪnæns tʃɑrdʒ/ (finance charges)

BANKING

NOUN A **finance charge** is any fee charged for borrowing money.

○ *The finance charge is the total amount of interest charged over the term of the loan expressed in dollar terms.*

○ *Finance charges may be treated as a form of interest.*

fi|nan|cial in|stru|ment /fɪnænʃl ɪnstrəmənt/ (financial instruments)

GENERAL

NOUN A **financial instrument** is a document or contract that can be traded in a market, that represents an asset to one party and a liability or equity to the other.

○ *In finance, a margin is collateral that the holder of a financial instrument has to deposit to cover some or all of the credit risk of their counterparty.*

○ *A promissory note is a financial instrument made by the debtor stating that the debtor intends to pay the money he owes to the creditor in the specified period.*

fi|nan|cial state|ments /faɪnænʃl steɪtmənts/

CORPORATE

NOUN **Financial statements** are all of the reports that show how a company is performing for a certain period.

○ *The company belatedly reported a $6.2 million loss for the first nine months of last year, but hasn't filed any financial statements since.*

○ *Stated capital is the amount of cash declared by the business as capital in the financial statements of the company.*

first|round fi|nanc|ing /fɜrstraʊnd faɪnænsɪŋ/

INVESTMENT: VENTURE CAPITALISM

NOUN **First round financing** is the first time a new company raises money from investors.

○ *First-round financing sources for a startup include the majority of venture capitalists, commercial banks, and government assistance programs.*

○ *More experienced companies give up less ownership and control than early-stage ventures in first-round financing.*

---

fis|cal year /fɪskᵊl yɪər/ (**fiscal years**)

CORPORATE

NOUN A **fiscal year** is a period of twelve months, used by organizations in order to calculate their budgets, profits, and losses.

○ *The company is finalizing the budget for the coming fiscal year.*

○ *The report must be filed within 90 days after the end of the company's fiscal year.*

---

fixed ex|change rate /fɪkst ɪkstʃeɪndʒ reɪt/ (**fixed exchange rates**)

FOREIGN EXCHANGE

NOUN A **fixed exchange rate** is an exchange rate set by the government for foreign exchange.

○ *Fixed exchange rates can help create stability in developing countries with weak financial institutions, but can lead to financial crisis in the long run.*

○ *In a fixed exchange rate system, exchange rates are either held constant or allowed to fluctuate only within very narrow boundaries.*

---

fixed rate /fɪkst reɪt/ (**fixed rates**)

BANKING

NOUN A **fixed rate** is an interest rate that is set to remain the same for the term of a loan.

○ *With a two-step mortgage, the borrower receives a fixed rate for a specified number of years, and then a new interest rate based on the terms in the note.*

○ *Money is lent to you for a fixed period, at a fixed rate of interest and repayments are calculated at the start of the loan.*

---

float /floʊt/ (**floats, floated, floating**)

INVESTMENT: VENTURE CAPITALISM

VERB If you **float** a company, you sell shares in it to the public.

○ *He floated his firm on the stock market.*

○ *In total, staff members own 40 percent of the company's shares and they didn't take any money off the table when the company floated.*

---

float|ing rate /floʊtɪŋ reɪt/ (**floating rates**)

FOREIGN EXCHANGE

NOUN A **floating rate** is an exchange rate for foreign exchange that is set by the trading market.

○ *Fixed-for-floating swaps in different currencies are used to convert a fixed rate asset in one currency to a floating rate asset in a different currency.*

○ *The exchange rate system is based on a dual official exchange rate structure: the floating rate and the export rate.*

---

fore|cast /fɔrkæst/ (**forecasts**)

ECONOMICS

NOUN A **forecast** is a prediction of future performance and financial position.

○ *External sales forecasts are based on historical experience, statistical analysis, and consideration of various macroeconomic factors.*

○ *The profit was in excess of the prospectus forecast.*

---

fore|clo|sure /fɔrkloʊʒər/ (**foreclosures**)

MORTGAGE

NOUN **Foreclosure** is the act of a lender, especially a mortgage lender, taking the collateral on a loan when loan payments are not made.

○ *If you do not make your mortgage payments, the bank will put your house into foreclosure.*

○ *Sales of a home from foreclosure proceedings are used to pay off the loans in the order they were recorded.*

---

for|ex /fɔrɛks/ (short for **foreign exchange**)

FOREIGN EXCHANGE

NOUN **Forex** is the market in which foreign currencies are traded.

○ *About 3 trillion dollars-worth of foreign exchange is traded globally every day, making forex larger than all bond markets put together.*

○ *Most Forex trade signals will likely include most major currencies like GBP, USD, and EUR.*

---

for|ward con|tracts /fɔrwərd kɒntrækts/

INVESTMENT

NOUN **Forward contracts** are agreements to buy something in the future for a price that has been agreed today.

○ *Since for most currencies the spot market value date is already 2 business days in the future, the shortest forward contracts are for a period of 3 days.*

○ *Buyers may enter forward contracts to purchase or sell currencies in the future at a rate of exchange agreed upon now.*

---

for|ward rate /fɔrwərd reɪt/ (**forward rates**)

FOREIGN EXCHANGE

NOUN The **forward rate** is the rate to exchange currency at a future date.

○ *The forward rate on this contract is the price you agree to pay in 6 months when the 100,000 euros are delivered.*

○ *Each variable rate payment is calculated based on the forward rate for each respective payment date.*

F|R|B /ɛf ɑr biː/ (short for **Federal Reserve Board**)

BANKING

ABBREVIATION The **FRB** is the board that governs the Federal Reserve system.

○ *The FRB dictates the amount of credit margin a brokerage or bank may lend to its customers.*

○ *The FRB is responsible for setting reserve requirements and the discount rate, and making other key economic decisions.*

Fred|die Mac /frɛdi mæk/ (short for **Federal Home Loan Mortgage Corporation**)

MORTGAGE

NOUN **Freddie Mac** is a US government corporation that buys and sells loans in order to provide mortgages to homebuyers.

○ Freddie Mac buys mortgages from lenders and resells them as securities on the secondary mortgage market.

○ The number of past due home loans guaranteed by Freddie Mac has fallen below the 4 percent threshold.

free cash flow /fri kæʃ floʊ/ (free cash flows)

CORPORATE

COUNT/NONCOUNT NOUN **Free cash flow** is revenue of a business that is available to spend.

○ Cash not retained and reinvested in the business is often known as free cash flow.

○ It is our goal to generate approximately $100 million in free cash flow.

front-end /frʌnt ɛnd/

GENERAL

ADJECTIVE **Front-end** costs are paid or charged before a project begins.

○ These investments are not subject to a front-end sales charge.

○ A mutual fund's prospectus includes complete information about applicable front-end sales charges.

fro|zen ac|count /froʊzən əkaʊnt/ (frozen accounts)

BANKING

NOUN A **frozen account** is a bank account that cannot have money withdrawn from it, because of a court order.

○ Funds may not be withdrawn from the frozen account until a lien is satisfied and a court order is received freeing the balance.

○ A frozen account is affected by a court order, with the consequence that no money may be deposited or withdrawn.

func|tion|al cur|ren|cy /fˈʌŋkʃənᵊl kɜrənsi/ (**functional currencies**)

FOREIGN EXCHANGE

NOUN A **functional currency** is the main currency used by a business.

○ If an item is denominated in the functional currency of the foreign operation, an exchange difference arises.

○ A British subsidiary of a US parent firm will declare that the pound is its functional currency, into which any foreign-currency income is translated.

fund /fˈʌnd/ (**funds**)

INVESTMENT

NOUN A **fund** is money from many different investors combined and invested in many different types of securities.

○ Net asset value is the value of a fund's investments.

○ In order to sell shares, an investor generally sells the shares back to the fund.

> **TYPES OF FUND**
>
> closed-end fund, hedge fund, mutual fund, pension fund, sinking fund

fund man|ag|er /fˈʌnd mænɪdʒər/ (**fund managers**)

INVESTMENT

NOUN A **fund manager** is a person that makes the investment decisions for a fund.

○ The pooled investment will be managed by a professional fund manager.

○ The structure of the deal can determine whether the fund manager can make a rapid investment decision or not.

> **PEOPLE IN FINANCE**
>
> Other names of people in finance include:
>
> backer, bondholder, certified public accountant, fiduciary, settlement agent, venture capitalist

fu|tures /fyu̱tʃərz/

INVESTMENT

NOUN **Futures** are contracts to buy something at a future date at a price that is agreed upon today.

○ The seller can offset risk by purchasing a futures contract to fix the sales price of the asset approximately.

○ The purchase or sale of a futures contract represents an obligation to accept or deliver an underlying asset at a price determined when the contract is executed.

Gg

GAAP /gæp/ (short for **generally accepted accounting principles**)

CORPORATE

ABBREVIATION In the US, **GAAP** are rules to which financial statements
of publicly traded companies must conform.

○ *Many insurance companies, particularly mutuals, do not report their data in GAAP terms.*

○ *The company needs to refinance a $2.65 billion loan on which it is now in default because its accounts no longer comply with GAAP standards.*

PRONUNCIATION

Note that this abbreviation is pronounced as a single word rather
than as individual letters. There are many abbreviations used in
finance that are also pronounced as words, including the
following:
CHIPS /tʃɪps/
FICO /faɪkoʊ/
LIBOR /laɪbɔr/
PITI /pɪti/
SWIFT /swɪft/

---

gain on sale /geɪn ɒn seɪl/ (**gains on sale**)

INVESTMENT

NOUN A **gain on sale** is the amount of money that is made by a company
when selling a non-inventory asset for more than its value.

○ *Other income and expense consists primarily of interest expense, interest income, and gain on sale of stock of a third party.*

○ *At the end of the accounting period, any gain on sale of securities must be included on the income statement.*

gain on trans|la|tion /geɪn ɒn trænzleɪʃᵊn/ (gains on translation)

FOREIGN EXCHANGE

NOUN A **gain on translation** is the amount of money that is made by a company by converting another currency used in a transaction into the functional currency of the company.

○ A gain on translation is recorded for a loan payable denominated in a foreign currency when the dollar has increased in value compared to the foreign currency.

○ The US dollar weakened, resulting in a gain on translation.

G|D|P /dʒi di pi/ (short for gross domestic product)

ECONOMICS

ABBREVIATION **GDP** is the total value of all the goods and services that a country produces or provides in a particular year, not including income from investments in other countries.

○ In the first quarter, GDP grew at an annual rate of more than 5 percent on the back of strong domestic demand.

○ It has taken an incredible amount of debt and money to obtain GDP growth over the past decade.

> **RELATED WORDS**
>
> Compare **GDP** with **GNP**, which is the total value of all the goods and services that a country produces or provides in a particular year, including income from investments in other countries.

Gin|nie Mae /dʒɪni meɪ/ (short for Government National Mortgage Association)

MORTGAGE

NOUN **Ginnie Mae** is a US government organization that buys mortgages from banks with money raised from selling government-backed securities.

○ Ginnie Mae differs from its related bodies in that it only purchases loans backed by the federal government.

○ *Ginnie Mae guarantees investors the full and timely payment of principal and interest on their mortgage backed securities.*

G|N|P /dʒi ɛn pi/ (short for **gross national product**)

ECONOMICS

ABBREVIATION **GNP** is the total value of all the goods and services that a country produces or provides in a particular year, including income from investments in other countries.

○ *The preliminary estimate of the second-quarter GNP showed good growth.*

○ *GNP is a measure of a nation's aggregate economic output.*

---

go bust /goʊ bʌst/

CORPORATE

PHRASE If a company **goes bust**, it loses so much money that it is forced to close down.

○ *Since the start of the recession, many well-known retailers have gone bust.*

○ *He invested in and briefly served on the board of a subprime mortgage lender that later went bust amid accounting problems.*

---

go|ing con|cern /goʊɪŋ kənsɜrn/ (**going concerns**)

CORPORATE

NOUN A **going concern** is a business that is not in danger of failing.

○ *The auditor was worried about whether the bank would be a going concern in 12 months' time.*

○ *Asset based lenders typically analyze a target company's viability as a going concern and its ability to service debt from cash flow.*

---

gold|en par|a|chute /goʊldᵊn pærəʃut/ (**golden parachutes**)

CORPORATE

NOUN A **golden parachute** is a very large payment and benefits that are offered to executives as part of their employment agreement if they are forced to leave a company.

○ Many of the sacked executives will collect a large golden parachute payment with their redundancy letter.

○ Without the golden parachute, managers may have some incentive to acquiesce too easily to strong, hostile takeover bids.

---

go long /goʊ lɔŋ/

INVESTMENT: STOCKS

PHRASE If an investor **goes long** on a stock, they bet that it will go up in price by purchasing it now and selling it later.

○ Both hedgers and speculators go long in the assets they expect to increase in value.

○ Whether daytrading or going long, nobody wants to buy into a dollar stock that seems likely to decline.

---

good|will /gʊdwɪl/

CORPORATE

NOUN **Goodwill** is an intangible asset that is taken into account when the value of an enterprise is calculated, reflecting the company's reputation and its relationship with its customers.

○ A major factor in the third-quarter loss was the write-down of $143.6 million of goodwill.

○ Goodwill is the largest intangible asset on the company's balance sheet.

---

gov|ern|ment def|i|cit /gʌvərnmənt dɛfɪsɪt/ (**government deficits**)

ECONOMICS

NOUN A **government deficit** is a situation in which a government spends more money than it has.

○ They must find a means of financing foreign policy and entitlement programs while reducing the government deficit.

○ Last year the government deficit was 13 percent of the GDP.

Hh

hard cur|ren|cy /hɑrd kɜrənsi/ (hard currencies)

FOREIGN EXCHANGE

NOUN **Hard currency** is a reliable currency from a stable country that is widely accepted around the world.

○ The country still lacks factories to make the consumer goods people want or the hard currency to buy them.

○ The islands, which rely on tourism for hard currency, have been suffering badly from falling numbers of visitors.

hedge /hɛdʒ/ (hedges, hedged, hedging)

INVESTMENT

VERB If you **hedge**, you reduce risk when conducting a transaction by doing an opposite transaction.

○ Investors were plowing their funds into oil and other commodities to hedge against inflation.

○ Private companies owe more than half of the country's foreign debt, much of it consisting of loans which were not hedged against currency risks.

hedge fund /hɛdʒ fʌnd/ (hedge funds)

INVESTMENT

NOUN A **hedge fund** is an investment fund that invests large amounts of money using methods that involve a lot of risk.

○ Some hedge fund investors deliberately steer clear of funds that earn 87 percent returns; they prefer those who aim for a steadier 10–12 percent.

○ A hedge fund is a pool of money, largely unregulated by the government, invested aggressively for wealthy clients.

HE|LOC /hílɒk/ (short for **Home Equity Line of Credit**)
MORTGAGE

ABBREVIATION A **HELOC** is an additional loan secured by a residence as well as the original mortgage.

○ Homeowners take out a HELOC as a method to consolidate debt.

○ When a person takes out a HELOC loan and purchases something, this certainly adds to the money supply.

hold /hoʊld/
BANKING

NOUN If a bank places a **hold** on an account, the owner cannot take money out of it.

○ A hold had been placed on your checking account due to suspicion of fraudulent activity.

○ A hold may be placed on an account to limit or prohibit payments against the account for a variety of reasons.

hold|ing com|pa|ny /hoʊldɪŋ kʌmpəni/ (**holding companies**)
CORPORATE

NOUN A **holding company** is a company with controlling shareholdings in one or more other companies.

○ The holding company has more than 50 percent of the total voting power and has the control on the other company.

○ The existing management team, assisted by financial investors, created and financed a holding company that then borrowed debt to acquire the target company.

hos|tile take|o|ver /hɒstəl teɪkoʊvər/ (**hostile takeovers**)
CORPORATE

NOUN A **hostile takeover** is a takeover of one company by another where the management is opposed to the acquisition.

○ The company is considering a restructuring to ward off a hostile takeover attempt by two European shipping concerns.

○ *Faced with a hostile takeover bid from Simtec Inc., the company said it toughened its shareholder-rights plan.*

RELATED WORDS
More words connected with takeovers

A **black knight** is someone making an unwelcome takeover attempt of a company. A **poison pill** is a way of trying to stop a takeover by doing something to make the company worth much less if the takeover were successful. A **tender offer** is an offer to buy shares directly from shareholders at a higher than market price, that can be part of a takeover bid or a share repurchase.

---

h

Ii

I|BAN /aɪbæn/ (short for **International Bank Account Number**)

BANKING

ABBREVIATION An **IBAN** is an internationally used number for identifying bank accounts.

○ *The IBAN is an international standard that uniquely identifies the account number of a bank's customer.*

○ *If you provide the IBAN on your supplier's bank account, then we recommend that you also provide the BIC for that supplier's bank branch.*

I|M|F /aɪ ɛm ɛf/ (short for **International Monetary Fund**)

GENERAL

ABBREVIATION The **IMF** is an international agency that tries to promote trade and improve economic conditions in poorer countries.

○ *The IMF helps its members to tide over the balance of payments problems with supplying the necessary loans.*

○ *The latest projections from the IMF show a gloomier assessment than that produced in April.*

---

im|pair|ment /ɪmpɛərmənt/

GENERAL

NOUN Impairment is the situation when the current value of an asset is less than the historical cost.

○ *Banks were partly responsible for the impairment of their asset portfolios because of their imprudent lending and investment policies.*

○ *Asset impairment happens when the carrying amount of an asset is greater than the amount recoverable either through using or selling an asset.*

in|come state|ment /ɪnkʌm steɪtmənt/ (**income statements**)

CORPORATE

NOUN An **income statement** is a financial statement showing the revenues and expenses of a company over a period of time.

○ *If the firm has a deficit in its income statement, it must borrow, raise more equity, or divest itself of assets purchased in the past.*

○ *Members of the audit committee must be able to read and understand fundamental financial statements, including a company's balance sheet, income statement, and cash flow statement.*

in|dex /ɪndɛks/ (**indexes**)

INVESTMENT

NOUN An **index** is a grouping of the combined values of stocks or securities that is used to track changes over time.

○ *The Dow Jones Industrial Average is the best known US index of stocks.*

○ *The gauge is designed to predict future growth, so a jump in the index means the economy will likely continue to expand in the coming months.*

in|fla|tion /ɪnfleɪʃⁿn/

ECONOMICS

NOUN **Inflation** is the economic situation when prices are rising over time and money loses value.

○ *Inflation causes the purchasing power of money to differ from one time to another.*

○ *Median incomes have also been rising steadily over the past ten years while inflation (nationwide) has been relatively stable.*

TALKING ABOUT INFLATION

If inflation gets higher, it **rises**. If it gets much higher, it **soars**. If it gets lower, it **falls**.

Something that makes inflation slow down or fall **controls**, **combats**, or **curbs** it, and something that makes it get higher **fuels** it.

Inflation that is getting higher very quickly can be described as **galloping**, **rampant**, or **spiraling**.

in|i|tial pub|lic of|fer|ing (ABBR **IPO**) /ɪnɪʃ°l pʌblɪk ɔfərɪŋ/
(initial public offerings)

INVESTMENT: VENTURE CAPITALISM

NOUN An **initial public offering** is the first offering of stock when a company goes public.

○ *The company began an initial public offering of 1.5 million common shares at $9 each, or a total of $13.5 million.*

○ *In an initial public offering, underwriters priced 2.5 million shares at $14 each.*

in|sid|er trad|ing /ɪnsaɪdər treɪdɪŋ/

INVESTMENT

NOUN **Insider trading** is the act of illegally buying or selling securities based on confidential information not known to the general investing public.

○ *There are legal barriers to private information becoming public, as with insider trading laws.*

○ *Insider trading is the buying or selling of a company's stock by that company's management, board of directors, or persons holding more than 10 percent of a company's shares.*

▶ **SYNONYM:**
insider dealing

in|sol|ven|cy /ɪnsɒlv°nsi/

GENERAL

NOUN **Insolvency** is the state of not having enough money to pay your debts.

○ *The cash flow projections allow you to plan your liquidity needs and identify difficult periods so that you can prepare for them and avoid the risk of insolvency.*

○ *When the business is threatened with insolvency, investors will deduct the goodwill from any calculation of residual equity because it will likely have no resale value.*

> **WORD BUILDER**
> **in-** = not
>
> The prefix **in-** is often added to adjectives to make their opposites: **insolvency**, **insolvent**, **intangible**.

in|sol|vent /ɪnsɒlvᵊnt/

GENERAL

ADJECTIVE If you are **insolvent**, you do not have enough money to pay your debts.

○ *The company was unable to pay its debts and was declared insolvent.*

○ *He was required to declare himself an insolvent debtor.*

in|stall|ment sales (BRIT **instalment sales**) /ɪnstɔlmənt seɪlz/

GENERAL

NOUN Installment sales are sales where fixed payments will be made regularly over a particular period of time.

○ *Taxes on installment sales are deferred until all payments are collected.*

○ *In installment sales, the purchaser agrees to pay for the purchase in a series of periodic payments.*

in|tan|gi|ble /ɪntændʒɪbᵊl/

GENERAL

ADJECTIVE A business asset that is **intangible** is not physical but it has a value, such as a trademark or copyright ownership.

○ *A good reputation is an intangible asset of immense financial worth.*

○ *Assets such as patents, trademarks, or goodwill are known as intangible assets in contrast to the physical ones such as plant and machinery.*

WORD BUILDER
-ible/-able = able to be done

The suffix **-ible** or **-able** often appears in adjectives that mean that a particular thing can be done to something: **convertible**, **intangible**, **marketable**, **negotiable**, **payable**.

---

in|tel|lec|tu|al prop|er|ty (ABBR **IP**) /ɪntɪlɛktʃuəl prɒpərti/

GENERAL

NOUN Intellectual property is something such as an invention or a copyright that is officially owned by someone.

○ *If there is to be innovation, the firm insists, intellectual property must be protected.*

○ *Music and films are defined as intellectual property, and owned by named individuals or companies.*

---

in|ter|bank rate /ɪntərbæŋk reɪt/ (**interbank rates**)
BANKING

NOUN The **interbank rate** is the interest rate that banks charge each other.

○ *The gap between the three-month interbank rate, at which banks lend to one another, and the base rate had opened up to an extraordinary extent last year.*

○ *The interbank rate of interest influences the base rate which is used by commercial banks to calculate rates of interest to be charged to their customers.*

---

in|ter|est /ɪntrɪst/
GENERAL

NOUN **Interest** is the extra money that you pay if you have borrowed money, or the extra money that you receive if you have money in some types of bank account.

○ *The home buyer puts up the other half of the closing costs and fee, and then pays interest at 12 percent a year to the investor.*

○ *Investors want to lend because lenders would typically receive the 10–15 percent interest on the loan.*

---

in|ter|est rate /ɪntrɪst reɪt/ (**interest rates**)
GENERAL

NOUN The **interest rate** is the amount of interest that must be paid on a loan or investment, expressed as a percentage of the amount that is borrowed or gained as profit.

○ *The Federal Reserve lowered interest rates by half a point.*

○ *Usually, short-term interest rates are lower than long-term rates, because investors want higher rates the longer they lend their money.*

in|ter|est rate swap /ˈɪntrɪst reɪt swɒp/ (**interest rate swaps**)

INVESTMENT

NOUN An **interest rate swap** is a contract where two parties exchange the cash flow from interest rates.

○ By entering into an interest rate swap, the net result is that each party can swap their existing obligation for their desired obligation.

○ The company may enter into interest rate swap agreements to limit the effect of increases in the interest rates on any floating rate debt.

in|ter|im re|sults /ˈɪntərɪm rɪzˈʌlts/

CORPORATE

NOUN A company's **interim results** are the set of figures, published outside the regular times, that show whether it has achieved a profit or a loss.

○ Interim results released last month showed a 6 percent rise to $256m.

○ The interim results were at the higher end of market expectations for the six-month period.

in|ter|nal rate of re|turn (ABBR **IRR**) /ɪntˈɜrnᵊl reɪt əv rɪtˈɜrn/

GENERAL

NOUN The **internal rate of return** is the interest rate at which a project would break even.

○ Use the internal rate of return to assess the acceptability of independent projects.

○ The internal rate of return is defined as the rate of discount at which a project would have zero net present value.

in|ter|na|tion|al ac|count|ing stand|ards (ABBR **IAS**)
/ˌɪntɜrnˈæʃənᵊl əkˈaʊntɪŋ stˈændərdz/

CORPORATE

NOUN **International accounting standards** are a set of internationally-agreed principles and procedures relating to the way that companies present their accounts.

○ The World Bank is making its loans to some companies conditional on their adoption of international accounting standards.

○ The investors required financial statements prepared using international accounting standards.

---

in the mon|ey /ɪn ðə mʌni/

INVESTMENT

PHRASE If an investment is **in the money**, it would be profitable if it was sold.

○ A binary option is an option that is designed to pay a certain value if in the money or pay nothing if out of the money.

○ An option that is not in the money has no intrinsic value.

---

in|vest /ɪnvɛst/ (**invests, invested, investing**)

INVESTMENT

VERB If you **invest** your money, you put it into a business or a bank, to try to make a profit from it.

○ He invested millions of dollars in the business.

○ The total invested in hedge funds of every variety was about $1.3 trillion.

---

in|vest|ment¹ /ɪnvɛstmənt/ (**investments**)

INVESTMENT

NOUN An **investment** is an amount of money that you invest, or the thing that you invest it in.

○ Anthony made a $1 million investment in the company.

○ The venture, with an initial investment of $1.3 million from both the partners, will focus on providing solutions for the telecoms sector.

> **TALKING ABOUT AN INVESTMENT**
>
> If you invest money, you **make** an investment. A **risky** investment is one where there is a high chance of losing your money.
>
> The first investment a person or organization makes in something is their **initial** investment. If they get their money back, they **recoup** their investment.

in|vest|ment² /ɪnˈvɛstmənt/

INVESTMENT

NOUN **Investment** is the activity of investing money.

○ He said that the government must introduce tax incentives to encourage investment.

○ The government is very open to foreign investment in the airline.

> **TALKING ABOUT INVESTMENT**
>
> Something that causes people or organizations to invest money **attracts**, **boosts**, **encourages**, or **stimulates** investment, while something that makes them unlikely to invest money **deters** or **discourages** investment.
>
> **Long-term** investment is when money is invested for a long period of time, and **short-term** investment is when money is invested for a short period of time.
>
> A **return on** investment is a measure of profitability that is calculated by dividing net profit by total assets.

in|vest|ment bank /ɪnˈvɛstmənt bæŋk/ (**investment banks**)

BANKING

NOUN An **investment bank** is a bank that can underwrite and issue securities and engage in trading in financial instruments.

○ If the investment bank can sell the securities at a higher price than it paid the issuer, it makes a profit.

○ An investment bank handles the equity and debt issuance, as well as proprietary trading with its own capital.

in|voice /ˈɪnvɔɪs/ (**invoices**)

GENERAL

NOUN An **invoice** is a document issued by a seller to a buyer that lists the goods or services that have been supplied and says how much money the buyer owes for them.

○ The invoice will show the goods ordered and purchased, their quantity, their unit and total price, and any sales tax being charged on the purchase.

○ *Once the sales and marketing department allots the car, the finance department prints out the invoice for the dealer, and the car is delivered.*

I|R|A /aɪ ɑr eɪ/ (short for **Individual Retirement Account**)

INVESTMENT: RETIREMENT

ABBREVIATION An **IRA** is a retirement account that allows a person to set aside a certain amount of money each year, with the tax on the earnings deferred until withdrawals begin.

○ *An IRA is an account which allows an investor to defer taxes while investing into the account.*

○ *An IRA can be used for retirement planning.*

I|S|I|N /aɪ ɛs aɪ ɛn/ (short for **International Securities Identification Number**)

INVESTMENT

ABBREVIATION An **ISIN** is a unique code that identifies a security.

○ *The clearing system will allocate a unique identification code, known as the ISIN, to each Eurobond issue.*

○ *Only one ISIN is used to identify a company, regardless of the number of securities traded for any particular company.*

---

is|sue price /ɪʃu praɪs/

INVESTMENT: STOCKS

NOUN The **issue price** is the price at which shares are offered for sale when they first become available to the public.

○ *Shares in the company slipped below their issue price on their first day of trading.*

○ *Investors earn the difference between the discount issue price and the full face value paid at maturity.*

Jj

joint ac|count /dʒɔɪnt əkaʊnt/ (**joint accounts**)

BANKING

NOUN A **joint account** is a bank account that is jointly owned by two people together, for example a married couple, or a parent and child.

- ○ We both used to have checking accounts, but now that my wife is retired, we use one joint account.
- ○ In the case of a joint account, each may make withdrawals from the account independently.

---

joint ven|ture (ABBR **JV**) /dʒɔɪnt vɛntʃər/ (**joint ventures**)

INVESTMENT

NOUN A **joint venture** is an arrangement between two or more people or companies to work together for a particular purpose or on a particular project.

- ○ The different participants may have different shares in the joint venture, resulting in different levels of profit or loss.
- ○ The company formed a 50–50 joint venture with Metallics Universal to make turbines.

---

junk bonds /dʒʌŋk bɒndz/

INVESTMENT

NOUN **Junk bonds** are bonds with a high risk that they will not be paid back, but with the possibility of a high yield.

- ○ Compared to higher-quality debt securities, junk bonds involve greater risk of default or price changes due to changes in credit quality of the issuer.
- ○ Recent experience suggests that 10–15 percent of maturing junk bonds will default each year over that period.

Ll

lad|der /lǽdər/ (ladders, laddered, laddering)

INVESTMENT

VERB If you **ladder** investments, you buy a series of them that mature in sequence.

○ If you wish to hold several individual CDs, consider laddering your investments, spreading maturity dates evenly over three to five years.

○ Laddered dividends can be a good retirement income strategy.

---

lag|ging in|di|ca|tor /lǽgɪŋ ɪndɪkeɪtər/ (lagging indicators)

ECONOMICS

NOUN A **lagging indicator** is an economic indicator that changes following a change in the economy, such as unemployment.

○ It seems that unemployment has turned from being a lagging indicator, following economic activity, to a coincident indicator, turning up with it.

○ A lagging indicator only follows what has happened earlier in the economy, while a leading indicator gives early signs of what is going to happen in the economy later.

---

large-cap /lɑ̱rdʒ kæp/

INVESTMENT: STOCKS

ADJECTIVE A **large-cap** company or stock is a company or stock that is worth over $10 billion.

○ Investors who buy large-cap equity stocks, which are inherently more risky than long-term government bonds, require a greater return.

○ Large-cap stock is generally considered less volatile than stock in smaller companies.

L|B|O /ɛl bi oʊ/ (short for **leveraged buyout**)

CORPORATE

ABBREVIATION An **LBO** is a situation in which an individual or a group buys a company with borrowed money that they will pay back by selling the company's assets.

○ Some bankers and businessmen think Germany could be ripe for hostile takeovers and even LBOs.

○ The rise in LBO activity over the first boom and bust cycle could be attributed to both regulatory and economic factors.

lead|ing in|di|ca|tor /liːdɪŋ ɪndɪkeɪtər/ (**leading indicators**)

ECONOMICS

NOUN A **leading indicator** is an economic indicator that changes before a change in the economy, and that can be used to predict future economic or financial activity.

○ As the leading indicator of future expenditures for construction work in progress, the current stability of contracting for new projects implies continued high-level spending ahead.

○ The Dow is the leading indicator of the stock market, and is a composite of 30 large industrial stocks.

lease-back /liːs bæk/ (**lease-backs**)

GENERAL

NOUN A **lease-back** is an agreement in which one person or company sells property to another, who then leases the property back to the seller.

○ When the lessor acquires the asset from the user and then leases it back to them, it is known as a sale and lease-back.

○ The buyers will receive lease-back guarantees of 9 percent of the apartment price annually for two years.

lease with op|tion to buy /liːs wɪð ɒpʃən tə baɪ/ (**leases with option to buy**)

GENERAL

NOUN A **lease with option to buy** is a lease that states that the person leasing the property has the right to purchase it at the end of the lease period.

○ If you're ready to buy a house, but your credit or savings aren't quite ready yet, a lease with option to buy may help you move in.

○ The agreement is a lease with option to buy, so you can rent it for $1850 a month, and $400 of the rent goes toward the purchase price of your option.

let|ter of cred|it (ABBR **LC**) /lɛtər əv krɛdɪt/ (**letters of credit**)

BANKING

NOUN A **letter of credit** is a letter written by a bank authorizing another bank to pay someone a sum of money.

○ If a seller agrees to be paid by a letter of credit, then you need a reliable bank to handle the transaction.

○ The project is being backed by a letter of credit from Lasalle Bank.

lev|er|age /lɛvərɪdʒ/

CORPORATE

NOUN **Leverage** is the amount of borrowed money that a company uses to run its business.

○ Converting either of those two securities into debt would only further raise the debt leverage of the buyout.

○ Financial leverage is usually measured by the ratio of long-term debt to total long-term capital.

LI|BOR /laɪbɔr/ (short for **London Interbank Offered Rate**)

BANKING

ABBREVIATION **LIBOR** is the interest rate that banks charge each other for large short-term loans.

○ The loan is to be repaid in 10 half-yearly installments at an effective interest rate of LIBOR plus 1 percent per annum.

○ *The loan bears interest at the LIBOR rate plus 200 basis points.*

---

lien /liːn/ (liens)

MORTGAGE

NOUN A **lien** is a legal claim on a piece of property that must be paid off before the property can be sold.

○ *If a court decides that a person must repay a debt, a lien may be placed against that person's property.*

○ *The seller may obtain clear title by paying the contractor and removing the lien.*

---

lim|it|ed part|ner|ship /lɪmɪtɪd pɑːtnərʃɪp/ (limited partnerships)

CORPORATE

NOUN A **limited partnership** is a form of partnership in which some of the partners contribute only financially and are liable only to the extent of the amount of money that they have invested.

○ *In a limited partnership structure, limited partners are shielded to the extent of their investment.*

○ *Usually, the limited partnership has a general partner who has unlimited liability but allows other partners to limit their potential loss.*

---

line of cred|it /laɪn əv krɛdɪt/ (lines of credit)

BANKING: CREDIT

NOUN A **line of credit** is a loan with a fixed maximum amount that a borrower may borrow without a fixed length of time or fixed payments.

○ *Once a business becomes established, and builds a high credit rating, it is often cheaper to draw on a commercial paper than on a bank line of credit.*

○ *Some lenders will let you skip a month on your mortgage payment or make an interest-only payment on your home line of credit.*

---

liq|uid as|sets /lɪkwɪd æsɛts/

GENERAL

NOUN **Liquid assets** are assets that can be easily converted into cash.

○ A company's most liquid assets are its holdings of cash and marketable securities.

○ Broker-dealers must have at all times enough liquid assets to promptly satisfy the claims of customers if the broker-dealer goes out of business.

---

li|quid|i|ty /lɪkwɪdɪti/
GENERAL

NOUN A company's **liquidity** is its ability to turn its assets into cash.

○ The company maintains a high degree of liquidity.

○ One way to ensure liquidity is to maintain large cash balances or arrange necessary borrowing facilities but neither approach results in optimal profitability.

---

li|quid|i|ty e|vent /lɪkwɪdɪti ɪvɛnt/ (**liquidity events**)
INVESTMENT: VENTURE CAPITALISM

NOUN A **liquidity event** is something that causes investors to receive proceeds for their equity, such as a merger, acquisition, or sale.

○ A liquidity event enables an investor to cash out or exit the investment by turning the investment into cash or marketable securities.

○ If suddenly many sellers want to sell a security because they experienced a liquidity event, the price of a security will drop to attract buyers.

L|L|C /ɛl ɛl si/ (short for **limited liability company**)
CORPORATE

ABBREVIATION An **LLC** is a form of company that limits the amount of liability undertaken by the company's shareholders.

○ The organization will be incorporated as an LLC corporation which will shield the owner and the three outside investors from issues of personal liability and double taxation.

○ An advantage of an LLC is that none of the owners are personally liable for its debts.

L|L|P /ɛl ɛl piː/ (short for **limited liability partnership**)

CORPORATE

ABBREVIATION An **LLP** is a type of partnership that limits the amount of liability undertaken by the partners to the amount that they have invested in the partnership.

○ An LLP can be a way to invest in real estate rentals with less risk.

○ An LLP differs from a limited partnership in that it has no general partner, only limited partners.

lock|box /lɒkbɒks/ (**lockboxes**)

BANKING

NOUN A **lockbox** is a bank account set up to receive payments from customers.

○ A company can use a lockbox service, whereby the bank receives and processes checks on its behalf.

○ A lockbox is an arrangement under which payments are mailed to a post office box that is serviced by a bank.

loss on sale /lɔs ɒn seɪl/ (**losses on sale**)

INVESTMENT

NOUN A **loss on sale** is the amount of money that is lost by a company when selling a non-inventory asset for more than its value.

○ The current cost net book value is $7200, so if the asset is being sold for $5000, there is a resulting loss on sale of $2200.

○ The sale price of the car is below its original cost, so there will be a loss on sale.

loss on trans|la|tion /lɔs ɒn trænzleɪʃᵊn/ (**losses on translation**)

FOREIGN EXCHANGE

NOUN A **loss on translation** is the amount of money that is lost by a company by converting another currency used in a transaction into the functional currency of the company.

○ If the exchange rate increases beyond this rate on the date of withdrawal, the additional loss on translation of liability will be debited to the profit and loss account.

○ When an entity translates their foreign currency into the functional currency of their enterprise, any resulting loss on translation should be recognized in an entity's profit and loss account.

L|T|V /ɛl ti vi/ (short for **loan to value ratio**)

BANKING

ABBREVIATION   **LTV** is the ratio of the value of an asset to the amount of money that a bank will lend in order to buy it.

○ In some cases it is possible to have 100 percent LTV of the purchase price of a property if you are able to buy at below market value.

○ Higher LTV ratios are primarily reserved for borrowers with higher credit scores and a satisfactory mortgage history.

L

Mm

---

make a mar|ket /meɪk ə mɑrkɪt/

INVESTMENT: STOCKS

PHRASE If you **make a market**, you hold a large enough percentage of a stock to be able to change its price.

○ *Dealing via brokers is more expensive than direct exchange, and larger banks try to make a market between themselves before engaging a broker's services.*

○ *Closely held companies issuing options must decide on how to make a market for them once they are exercised.*

---

mar|gin /mɑrdʒɪn/ (margins)

INVESTMENT: STOCKS

NOUN If you buy stocks **on the margin**, you borrow money in order to buy them, in the hope that they will increase in value before you have to pay the loan back.

○ *The government expanded the scope of permissible capital market activities, such as allowing finance companies to fund equity purchases on the margin.*

○ *People are borrowing on credit cards to gamble on the margin, so that they quickly climb into serious debt to try to recoup losses.*

---

mar|gin call /mɑrdʒɪn kɔl/ (margin calls)

INVESTMENT: STOCKS

NOUN A **margin call** is a situation in which the broker who offered the ability to buy on the margin demands additional funds to make up for a loss in the margin account.

○ *If the security falls and the investor's margin falls, the investor is at risk for a margin call.*

○ *When the price of a stock rises significantly, some people may be forced to close their position to meet a margin call.*

mar|ket|a|ble se|cu|ri|ties /mɑrkɪtəbᵊl sɪkyʊərɪtiz/

INVESTMENT: STOCKS

NOUN **Marketable securities** are securities that can easily be sold quickly on the open market.

○ Assets that can be converted into cash immediately usually include bank accounts and marketable securities, such as government bonds and banker's acceptances.

○ The increase in tax benefits was due to an increase in tax-exempt interest income from the company's marketable securities.

mar|ket cap /mɑrkɪt kæp/ (market caps)

INVESTMENT: STOCKS

NOUN A **market cap** is the total market value of all the shares in a company.

○ A company's market cap is calculated by multiplying its current share price by the number of shares outstanding.

○ The company has been a resounding success, with revenues of $5.60 million, and a market cap of $5.50 billion.

mark-to-mar|ket /mɑrk tə mɑrkɪt/

CORPORATE

PHRASE **Mark-to-market** is the process of adjusting the value of an asset on the balance sheet to reflect the current market price, instead of the historical cost.

○ Mark-to-market accounting meant that banks were valuing illiquid assets at prices which reflected a lack of buyers as much as underlying credit quality.

○ There is fierce criticism against mark-to-market accounting from the banks.

ma|tur|i|ty /mətyʊərɪti/

INVESTMENT

NOUN **Maturity** is the time when an investment or insurance will be paid back.

○ Changes in interest rates have greater impact on funds with longer average maturity.

○ The retail investor is simply not interested in trading; he prefers to hold investments till maturity and earn income.

mer|chant ac|count /mɜrtʃənt əkaʊnt/ (**merchant accounts**)

BANKING: CREDIT

NOUN A **merchant account** is a type of bank account that allows a company to accept credit cards.

○ *Getting a merchant account to handle credit card payments may be your best long-term solution to the problem of getting paid.*

○ *If you are taking credit card details over a website, you will need a merchant account with a reputable bank to process the payments.*

mer|ger /mɜrdʒər/ (**mergers**)

CORPORATE

NOUN A **merger** is the joining together of two separate companies or organizations so that they become one.

○ *The merger of two firms lessens the probability of default on either firm's debt.*

○ *The advantages from the merger could allow the new company to emerge a low-cost producer.*

> **TALKING ABOUT MERGERS**
>
> A **proposed** merger is a merger that has been suggested. Two companies may **announce** a merger.
>
> If a merger is **approved**, it is allowed to happen, and if it is **blocked**, it is not allowed to happen.
>
> Two companies trying to reach an agreement to merge are **negotiating** a merger.

MI|CR en|cod|ing /mɪkər ɪnkoʊdɪŋ/ (short for **magnetic ink character recognition encoding**)

BANKING

NOUN The **MICR encoding** of a check is the magnetic ink pattern at the bottom that can be scanned and that contains information about the check.

○ *The MICR encoding is found in the lower right corner of the check, with the check amount.*

○ *MICR encoding is printed on transaction items such as checks and deposit tickets and read by computers or optical scanners for rapid processing of the items.*

---

mid|cap /mɪd kæp/

INVESTMENT: STOCKS

ADJECTIVE A **mid-cap** company or stock is a company or stock that is worth between $2 billion and $10 billion.

○ *Investing primarily in mid-cap companies is likely to involve a higher degree of liquidity risk and price volatility than investments in larger capitalization securities.*

○ *Mid-cap stocks tend to have less volatility than small-cap stocks, but more volatility than large-cap stocks.*

---

mod|i|fi|ca|tion /mɒdɪfɪkeɪʃᵊn/ (modifications)

MORTGAGE

NOUN A **modification** is a change to the terms of a loan that have previously been agreed.

○ *The terms of loans may be regulated, with modifications from time to time so as to discourage or encourage new borrowing.*

○ *Many homeowners have reported that their lenders won't give them a mortgage modification unless they're behind on their payments.*

> **WORD BUILDER**
> **-ation** = action
>
> The suffix **-ation** often appears in nouns that relate to the action of the verb they are formed from: **allocation**, **capitalization**, **demutualization**, **depreciation**, **diversification**, **modification**, **speculation**, **translation**, **valuation**.

---

mon|ey mar|ket /mʌni mɑrkɪt/ (money markets)

INVESTMENT

NOUN The **money market** is investments in safe short-term securities.

○ To receive the money before the bill is due, the creditor can get the bill accepted by a commercial bank, and it can then be sold on the money market for a small discount.

○ Already, corporates have been allowed to park their short-term surpluses in money market instruments.

mon|ey sup|ply /mʌni səplaɪ/

ECONOMICS

NOUN The **money supply** is the amount of money in circulation.

○ Current US policy is to provide for expanding the money supply through lending for as long as can be accomplished.

○ The high growth in money supply is largely attributable to the growth in bank credit to the government.

mu|ni bonds /myuni bɒndz/ (short for **municipal bonds**)

INVESTMENT

NOUN **Muni bonds** are bonds issued by local municipal governments on which the interest is often tax-free.

○ State or local governments offer muni bonds to pay for special projects such as highways or sewers.

○ Muni bonds have usually yielded slightly less than Treasury debt, thanks to a tax exemption on interest income and a reputation for safety.

mu|tu|al fund /myutʃuəl fʌnd/ (**mutual funds**)

INVESTMENT

NOUN A **mutual fund** is an investment where many people buy shares, and a professional manager invests the money in a diverse portfolio.

○ A balanced fund is a mutual fund that invests in common stocks, preferred stocks, bonds and short-term fixed income securities.

○ If you are too busy to actively manage your own portfolio or not too sure of picking the best stocks, the mutual fund is a safe bet.

Nn

NAF|TA /ˈnæftə/ (short for **North American Free Trade Agreement**)

ECONOMICS

ABBREVIATION **NAFTA** is an agreement between the US, Canada, and Mexico that allows them to trade with each other without paying import taxes.

○ *Since it came into force, NAFTA has benefited all three economies, raising cross-border trade and investment.*

○ *NAFTA created an established order in the new relationship with America and Canada, with a specific timetable for the opening of most key industries.*

NAS|DAQ /ˈnæzdæk/ (short for **National Association of Securities Dealers Automated Quotation**)

INVESTMENT: STOCKS

ABBREVIATION **NASDAQ** is a US computerized system for trading stocks, especially stocks of high-technology companies.

○ *The NASDAQ system automated order processing and provided brokers with the latest competitive price quotes via a computer terminal.*

○ *The NASDAQ stock market dropped 83.9 points and the dot-com bubble began to burst.*

na|tion|al bank /ˈnæʃənᵊl bæŋk/ (**national banks**)

BANKING

NOUN A **national bank** is a bank in the US that is regulated by the OCC.

○ *A commercial bank obtains a charter either from the Comptroller of the Currency in the case of a national bank or from a state banking authority in the case of a state bank.*

○A national bank may charge the maximum rate of interest permitted by state law for any state-chartered or state-licensed lending institution.

TYPES OF BANK

The following are all types of bank:

commercial bank, correspondent bank, custodian bank, investment bank

---

na|tion|al debt /næʃənªl dɛt/

ECONOMICS

NOUN A country's **national debt** is the amount of debt owed by the government of that country.

○Congress imposes a ceiling on the total national debt, but can raise it when accumulated debt approaches the ceiling.

○The primary factor will be a rise in inflation rates greatly above today's levels, caused by the government's attempts to manage the national debt.

N|C|U|A /ɛn si yu eɪ/ (short for **National Credit Union Administration**)

BANKING

ABBREVIATION The **NCUA** is a US government agency that monitors federal credit unions.

○The NCUA charters and examines the books of federally chartered credit unions and imposes restrictions on assets they can hold.

○The Boeing Employees Credit Union is insured by the NCUA.

---

ne|go|tia|ble /nɪɡoʊʃiəbªl/

GENERAL

ADJECTIVE A **negotiable** asset is able to be transferred legally from one owner to another.

○Negotiable paper is a document that can be traded for value by its holder independently of the parties that created it.

○Negotiable paper can be used to pay debts.

net pre|sent val|ue (ABBR **NPV**) /nɛt prɛzənt vælyu/

INVESTMENT

NOUN The **net present value** of an investment or project is all the income that it can be expected to produce minus all the costs, taking into account the future value of this income and these costs.

○ *Losses or negative returns must get subtracted from future profits or gains to calculate the net present value of the company to investors.*

○ *If the net present value of the project is above zero, the project is likely to be profitable.*

no-load /noʊ loʊd/

INVESTMENT

ADJECTIVE A **no-load** fund is a fund sold directly by the investment company with no fees or commissions.

○ *A true no-load fund has neither a sales charge nor a distribution fee to purchase shares.*

○ *A no-load fund may still charge account fees.*

nos|tro ac|count /nɒstroʊ əkaʊnt/ (**nostro accounts**)

BANKING

NOUN A **nostro account** is an account that a bank holds with another bank in a foreign country in the foreign currency. "Nostro" is from the Latin "noster," meaning "our."

○ *A nostro account is maintained by an Indian Bank in the foreign countries for the easy clearing of their transactions.*

○ *If the bank pays a demand drawn on it by its correspondent bank, the correspondent bank credits the nostro account of the paying bank while issuing the demand draft.*

WORD ORIGINS
Latin words

Several other financial terms include Latin words. A **vostro account** is an account that a domestic bank holds for another foreign bank in the domestic bank's currency. "Vostro" is from the Latin "voster," meaning "your."

> **Ad valorem** is an adjective that describes a tax charged at the estimated value of the goods being charged, and is the Latin for "according to value," and in the phrase **cum dividend**, "cum" means "with," so investors who buy shares cum dividend are entitled to a recently issued dividend.

note pay|a|ble /no͞ut pe͟ɪəbᵊl/ (notes payable)

GENERAL

NOUN A **note payable** is a written legal obligation to repay an amount of borrowed money at a particular future date.

○ As of June 30, the company had $338.8 million in short-term debt, including notes payable of $83.6 million.

○ The company had $333,617 outstanding under a long-term note payable to a bank.

N|S|F /ɛn ɛs ɛf/ (short for **not sufficient funds**)

BANKING

ABBREVIATION A check where there is not enough money in the account to pay for it will be marked **NSF**.

○ NSF checks may be rejected by the bank, or, alternatively, the bank customer may set up an overdraft loan account, which will cover these checks.

○ A check that bounces is often called NSF.

N|Y|S|E /ɛn waɪ ɛs i/ (short for **New York Stock Exchange**)

INVESTMENT: STOCKS

ABBREVIATION The **NYSE** is the main stock market in the US.

○ A stock exchange based in New York, the NYSE is also known as the Big Board.

○ Over the next six months, we will see several manufacturing and services companies seeking listing on the NYSE.

n

Oo

O|C|C /<u>ou</u> si si/ (short for **Office of the Comptroller of the Currency**)

ECONOMICS

ABBREVIATION The **OCC** is a federal agency that is responsible for monitoring all national banks, and federal branches and agencies of foreign banks.

○ The OCC supervises the capital adequacy of national banks and federal branches of foreign banking organizations.

○ The OCC initially had the power to charter national banks that could issue national banknotes.

> **RELATED WORDS**
> **US agencies**
>
> Other US agencies include **NCUA**, the National Credit Union Association that monitors federal credit unions, and the **SEC**, the Securities and Exchange Commission, responsible for regulating the financial reporting of companies whose stock is publicly traded.

---

of|fer /ɔfər/ (**offers**)

GENERAL

NOUN An **offer** is the amount of money that someone says they will pay to buy something.

○ The company accepted a takeover offer of $29.835 a share.

○ They made an offer for all shares outstanding and it was approved by 80 percent of holders.

> **TALKING ABOUT OFFERS**
>
> If you make an offer to someone, you **submit** it. The person or organization may **accept** the offer, or **decline**, **refuse**, or **reject** it.
>
> If you change an offer, you **revise** it, and if you say that you no longer wish to make the offer, you **withdraw** it.

---

o|pen-end|ed loan /oupən ɛndɪd loʊn/ (open-ended loans)

BANKING: CREDIT

NOUN An **open-ended loan** is an extension of credit where money can be borrowed when you need it, and paid back on an ongoing basis, such as a credit card.

○ An open-ended loan, such as a credit card account or line of credit, does not have a definite term or end date.

○ A credit card is a kind of open-ended loan, since the money is lent with no fixed end date.

---

op|por|tu|ni|ty cost /ɒpərtunɪti kɔst/ (opportunity costs)

ECONOMICS

NOUN An **opportunity cost** is the cost of not being able to do other things with time and resources because of doing the chosen activity.

○ The opportunity cost of holding money rather than buying bonds or some other interest-bearing asset is the nominal interest that would otherwise be earned.

○ The opportunity cost of holding money rather than investing it for interest is the nominal interest that would otherwise be earned.

---

op|tion /ɒpʃᵊn/ (options)

INVESTMENT: STOCKS

NOUN An **option** is an agreement or contract that gives someone the right to buy or sell a property or shares at a future date.

○ Each bank has granted the other an option on 19.9 percent of its shares.

○ Under the program, he still holds options to buy 42,000 shares at the same low rate.

out of the mon|ey /aʊt əv ðə mʌni/

INVESTMENT: STOCKS

PHRASE If an investment is **out of the money**, it would be a loss if it was sold.

○ *Usually, these options are designed to pay a certain value if in the money or pay nothing if out of the money.*

○ *When the strike price of a call option exceeds the current asset price, the call option is said to be out of the money.*

out|stand|ing /aʊtstændɪŋ/

BANKING

ADJECTIVE Money that is **outstanding** has not yet been paid and is still owed to someone.

○ *The total debt outstanding is $70 billion.*

○ *The company had 140.9 million shares outstanding in the latest quarter.*

o|ver|li|mit /oʊvərlɪmɪt/

BANKING: CREDIT

ADJECTIVE When more money has been charged on a credit card than is available as credit, the credit card is **overlimit**.

○ *Issuers cannot charge overlimit fees unless they have offered consumers the option of having a fixed credit limit that cannot be exceeded.*

○ *A credit card overlimit fee is charged when you exceed your credit limit, even if it's because of fees or interest.*

o|ver-the-coun|ter (ABBR **OTC**) /oʊvər ðə kaʊntər/

INVESTMENT: STOCKS

ADJECTIVE **Over-the-counter** shares are not bought and sold on a stock exchange, but directly with a broker.

○ *Securities companies were allowed to trade shares that were neither traded on an exchange nor registered as over-the-counter shares.*

○ *In national over-the-counter trading yesterday, the company's stock fell 25 cents to close at $16.75 a share.*

Pp

paid-in cap|i|tal /peɪd ɪn kæpɪtᵊl/

CORPORATE

NOUN **Paid-in capital** is the money a company has received from investors in return for issuing stock.

○ Paid-in capital arising from the sale of treasury stock should not be included in the measurement of net income.

○ When the price of new shares sold to the public exceeds the par value the difference is entered in the company's accounts as additional paid-in capital.

par /pɑr/

INVESTMENT: STOCKS

NOUN **Par** is the original issue price of a stock or bond.

○ Individual banks were required to accept each others' notes at par, which forced the free market out of banking as notes from distressed banks could no longer be discounted.

○ The company issued at par $10,000 of 6 percent bonds convertible in total into 1,000 shares of its common stock.

part|ner|ship /pɑrtnərʃɪp/ (partnerships)

CORPORATE

NOUN A **partnership** is a company that is owned by two or more people, who share in the risks and rewards of the business.

○ The department store operator said that buying the stake in the subsidiary is part of a broad agreement to form a partnership.

○ When the two companies merged, the bigger company became the dominant player in the partnership.

par val|ue /pɑr vælyu/ (par values)

INVESTMENT

NOUN **Par value** is the face value of a bond.

○ A price of 80 means that the bond is selling at 80 percent of its par value.

○ $1,800,000 of these bonds were converted into 500 shares of $20 par value common stock.

pay|day loan /peɪdeɪ loʊn/ (payday loans)

BANKING

NOUN A **payday loan** is a small personal cash loan at a very high interest rate, secured by the borrower's next paycheck.

○ A stipulation that payday loan providers frequently use to establish how much money you can borrow is how much you earn.

○ You can't talk about the annual percentage rate in terms of temporary loans as no one actually retains a payday loan for an entire year.

> **TYPES OF LOAN**
>
> bridge loan, closed-end loan, open-ended loan, payday loan, subprime loan

peg¹ /pɛg/ (pegs, pegged, pegging)

FOREIGN EXCHANGE

VERB If a currency is **pegged** to another currency, or to gold, its price is fixed in relation to the price of that currency or to gold.

○ The trade-weight value of the dollar is the value of the dollar pegged to a market basket of selected foreign currencies.

○ Naturally, as the dollar appreciated relative to the yen, so did those currencies pegged to it.

peg² /pɛg/ (short for **price/earnings to growth ratio**) (pegs)

INVESTMENT: STOCKS

NOUN The **peg** ratio is a ratio that is used to decide the value of a stock, while taking into account earnings growth.

○A high peg ratio indicates that the market is significantly more enthused about the growth prospects of a company than are analysts.

○The peg ratio for analyzing the value of stocks combines the forecast earnings for a stock as well as price and earnings.

---

pen|ny stocks /pɛni stɒks/

INVESTMENT: STOCKS

NOUN **Penny stocks** are high-risk stock that sells for a very low price outside of the main stock exchange.

○What distinguishes a company issuing penny stocks is that it has not yet developed into a stable business.

○The Vancouver exchange specializes in the risky, low-priced penny stocks of gold exploration concerns and other startup ventures.

---

pen|sion fund /pɛnʃ°n fʌnd/ (**pension funds**)

INVESTMENT: RETIREMENT

NOUN A **pension fund** is an investment fund for retirement plans.

○A pension fund provides a lump sum to purchase a pension in retirement.

○New Hampshire is among those to require that new workers contribute more of their salary to the pension fund.

> **TYPES OF PENSION**
>
> The following are types of retirement investments or accounts:
>
> 401(k), annuity, IRA, Roth IRA

---

pe|ri|od|ic rate /pɪəriɒdɪk reɪt/ (**periodic rates**)

BANKING

NOUN The **periodic rate** is the interest rate charged for each period, such as monthly or quarterly.

○The periodic rate on a credit card with an 18 percent annual percentage rate is 1.5 percent per month.

○The annual percentage rate is the periodic rate times the number of periods in a year.

pig|gy|back in|vest|ing /ˈpɪɡibæk ɪnvɛstɪŋ/

INVESTMENT

NOUN **Piggyback investing** is a situation in which a broker repeats a trade on his own behalf immediately after trading for an investor, because he thinks the investor may have inside information.

○ *Piggyback investing is trend-following behavior that is adopted by less informed investors as a way to profit from the bets of what are believed to be better-informed investors.*

○ *Piggyback investing is the art and science of building portfolios based on mimicking the stock picks of some of the best superinvestors.*

PIN /pɪn/ (short for **personal identification number**)

BANKING

ABBREVIATION A **PIN** is a secret number used to withdraw money from an ATM or to authorize a debit card.

○ *Usually when you use a debit card, you must key in a PIN.*

○ *Your PIN is the number that you use as a security access code for your bank accounts when you use telephone or Internet banking, or an ATM.*

PI|TI /pɪti/ (short for **principal, interest, taxes, and insurance**)

MORTGAGE

ABBREVIATION **PITI** is the components of a mortgage payment.

○ *When a buyer applies for a loan, the lender will calculate the PITI, which may be combined in a single monthly mortgage payment.*

○ *Lenders use PITI to calculate your monthly mortgage obligation and how much you can afford to borrow.*

P|M|I /pi ɛm aɪ/ (short for **private mortgage insurance**)

MORTGAGE

ABBREVIATION **PMI** is an insurance policy that protects the holder against loss resulting from default on a mortgage loan.

○ *Insurance requirements are sufficient to guarantee that the lender gets some pre-defined percentage of the loan value back, either from foreclosure auction proceeds or from PMI.*

○ *PMI is extra insurance that lenders require from most homebuyers who obtain loans that are more than 80 percent of their new home's value.*

---

poi|son pill /pɔɪzᵊn pɪl/ (**poison pills**)

CORPORATE

NOUN A **poison pill** is a way of trying to stop a takeover by doing something to make the company worth much less if the takeover were successful.

○ *Some believe this level of compensation is essentially a poison pill to put off any rival bidders.*

○ *The company adopted a poison pill technique to protect them against hostile takeovers.*

---

port|fo|li|o /pɔrtfoʊlioʊ/ (**portfolios**)

INVESTMENT: STOCKS

NOUN A **portfolio** is all of someone's investments together.

○ *You should ask to see a simplified presentation of the private equity firm's portfolio and the initial results of their investments, so you can judge their performance.*

○ *The investment manager will bring all the experience he has accumulated from the other businesses in his portfolio.*

---

post|date /poʊstdeɪt/ (**postdates, postdated, postdating**)

BANKING

VERB If you **postdate** a check or other document, you put a future date on it so that it is not valid until then.

○ *It is inadvisable for a payee to take a postdated check in satisfaction of an outstanding debt.*

○ *Postdated checks were used to make payment for a future date.*

▶ **COLLOCATION:**
postdate a check

P

pref|erred stock /prɪfɜ́rd stɒ́k/

INVESTMENT: STOCKS

NOUN **Preferred stock** is the shares in a company that are owned by people who have the right to receive part of the company's profits before the holders of common stock.

○ They approved the proposal to swap one share of preferred stock for 1.2 shares of common stock and one warrant to purchase another common share for $3.50 until June 30.

○ The options entitle the employees to purchase preferred stock at $50 per share.

pre|mi|um /prímiəm/ (premiums)

INVESTMENT

NOUN A **premium** is the higher price that is paid for a bond that is trading above par.

○ Yield to maturity takes into account the present value of all future cash flows, as well as any premium or discount to par that the investor pays.

○ If prices are above par, and the bond is priced at greater than 100, this is called trading at a premium.

pre|sent val|ue of fu|ture cash flows /prɛ́zənt vǽlyu əv fyútʃər kǽʃ floʊz/

ECONOMICS

NOUN The **present value of future cash flows** is a method of discounting cash that you expect to receive in the future to the value at the current time.

○ Information about the risks of any investment is used to derive a discount rate appropriate for estimating the present value of future cash flows, which is the basis of most asset pricing models.

○ If no comparable market prices exist, the present value of future cash flows should be used as a measure of fair value.

price earn|ings ra|ti|o (ABBR PE ratio) /praɪs ɜ́rnɪŋz reɪʃoʊ/

INVESTMENT: STOCKS

NOUN The **price earnings ratio** is the market price of common stock per share divided by earnings per share.

○ *The price earnings ratio is the most widely used valuation method, comparing the ratio of the current stock price to the current or projected earnings per share.*

○ *The price earnings ratio relates market values to company profits.*

---

prime /praɪm/

BANKING: CREDIT

ADJECTIVE **Prime** borrowers are the least risky, most creditworthy borrowers.

○ *The term "subprime" refers to the credit quality of particular borrowers, who have weakened credit histories and a greater risk of loan default than prime borrowers.*

○ *According to the Wall Street Journal, 61 percent of all subprime loans that year went to prime borrowers.*

> **RELATED WORDS**
>
> Compare with **subprime**. A subprime loan is a loan with a higher interest rate, to borrowers who are a high credit risk.

---

prime rate /praɪm reɪt/ (**prime rates**)

BANKING

NOUN A **prime rate** is the interest rate that banks give to their best customers such as large corporations.

○ *The prime rate, which is the interest rate the bank charges on loans to its most creditworthy customers, is adjusted up or down as interest rates on traded securities change.*

○ *The prime rate is a key interest rate for commercial lending.*

---

prin|ci|pal /prɪnsɪpᵊl/ (**principals**)

BANKING

NOUN A **principal** is the amount of money originally borrowed on a loan.

○ *The agreement gives bank creditors three basic options: cutting back interest payments, reducing debt principal, or lending further funds.*

○ *Investors have the choice of having not just the principal, but also the dividends cumulatively being converted into shares.*

pri|vate place|ment /praɪvɪt pleɪsmənt/ (**private placements**)

INVESTMENT: STOCKS

NOUN A **private placement** is the sale of securities to a small chosen group of investors in order to raise capital.

○ In the primary markets, securities may be offered to the public in a public offer, or alternatively, they may be offered privately to a limited number of qualified persons in a private placement.

○ Venture capital financing generally comes in the form of a private placement to one or more venture capital firms.

▶ SYNONYM:
non-public offering

pro|ceeds /prouʂidz/

GENERAL

NOUN The **proceeds** of an activity or the sale of something is the money and other assets received from it.

○ The company planned to use the proceeds from the sale to help pay the debt it would have incurred in its proposed $12 billion acquisition.

○ They reached an agreement that they won't pursue a claim to the proceeds of the planned sale.

prof|it mar|gin /prɒfɪt mɑrdʒɪn/ (**profit margins**)

CORPORATE

NOUN A **profit margin** is the difference between the selling price of a product and the cost of producing and marketing it.

○ The group had a net profit margin of 30% last year.

○ Firms have tended to increase their profit margins on existing volumes, rather than cut prices to increase their market share.

prof|it warn|ing /prɒfɪt wɔrnɪŋ/ (**profit warnings**)

CORPORATE

NOUN A **profit warning** is an announcement by a company that its profits will be much lower than had been expected.

○ Siemens issued a surprise profit warning because of delays to projects.

○ The leading PC maker issued a profit warning last week that sent its share price to a five-year low.

---

pro for|ma /proʊ fɔrmə/

CORPORATE

ADJECTIVE A company's **pro forma** balance or earnings are their expected balance or earnings.

○ Companies seeking debt financing usually draw up a set of pro forma income statements and balance sheets.

○ The company presented its pro forma earnings as if it had not lost $7 million investing in poor stocks.

▶ **COLLOCATIONS:**
pro forma balance
pro forma invoice
pro forma statement

---

prom|is|so|ry note /prɒmɪsɔri noʊt/ (**promissory notes**)

GENERAL

NOUN A **promissory note** is a written promise to pay a particular sum of money to someone by a particular date.

○ If an order is very large, the customer may be asked to sign a promissory note.

○ The borrower must signal their good faith by making a deposit or signing a promissory note or letter of credit guaranteed by the central bank.

---

pro ra|ta /proʊ reɪtə/

GENERAL

ADJECTIVE Something that is **pro rata** is allocated in proportion to its share of the whole.

○ Each company in the group pays its pro rata share of losses and expenses.

○ They are paid their salaries and are entitled to fringe benefits on a pro rata basis.

pro|spec|tus /prəspɛktəs/ (**prospectuses**)

INVESTMENT: STOCKS

NOUN A **prospectus** is a document issued by the SEC that gives detailed information about a stock offering for investors.

○ A prospectus is generally published by a company seeking to place a new issue of shares and is designed to give potential investors key facts about the company.

○ A prospectus is part of a registration statement filed with the SEC when offering securities.

prox|y /prɒksi/ (**proxies**)

INVESTMENT: STOCKS

NOUN A **proxy** is a person who is authorized to vote shares for shareholders who are not present.

○ Shareholders can and often do give management their proxies, delegating the right and responsibility to vote their shares as specified.

○ Delaware was one of the first states to allow voting by electronic proxy and attendance at stockholder meetings through the Internet.

pub|lic com|pa|ny /pʌblɪk kʌmpəni/ (**public companies**)

INVESTMENT: STOCKS

NOUN A **public company** is a company whose shares can be bought by the general public.

○ Shares in a public company can be bought and sold on the stock exchange and so can be bought by the general public.

○ A public company is usually defined as one whose shares are sold or issued to the public and which must have at least two directors.

RELATED WORDS
Types of company

A **startup** is a new company that is just beginning operations, and a **small-cap** company is worth under $1 billion.

A **corporation** is a large business or company.

A **partnership** is owned by two or more people. In a **limited partnership**, some of the partners contribute only financially and are liable only to the extent of the amount of money that they have invested. An **LLP**, or limited liability partnership, is a type of partnership that limits the amount of liability undertaken by the partners to the amount that they have invested in the partnership.

---

put /pʊt/ (puts)

INVESTMENT: STOCKS

NOUN A **put** is the right to sell something like a stock or commodity at a certain price.

○ *An ordinary put is an option given to a person to sell to the writer a specified amount of securities at a stated price within a certain time.*

○ *The gain or loss on a put is short or long term depending on the holding period of the stock involved.*

RELATED WORDS

Compare this with a **call**, which is the right to buy something like a stock or commodity at a certain price. A **straddle** is the act of purchasing both call and put options for the same investment.

P

Qq

quote /kwout/ (**quotes**)

INVESTMENT: STOCKS

NOUN A **quote** is the bid, ask, and list prices for a stock or bond or other security at a particular time.

- In the company's stock quote, the latest quarterly dividend would be recorded as $0.25 per share and the share price as $67.44.

- Investors who call the 888 number are instructed to use the phone key pad to get the latest stock quote, listen to a release, request a report or talk to an operator.

Rr

ra|men prof|it|a|ble /rɑmən prɒfɪtəblˀl/

INVESTMENT: VENTURE CAPITALISM

ADJECTIVE If a startup business is **ramen profitable**, it is barely profitable, just enough to allow the founder to live on the cheapest diet. This informal term describes a startup where only enough money to be able to afford the basic foodstuff ramen noodles is being made.

○ *An increasing number of single founders are managing to get their startups ramen profitable while maintaining 100 percent equity and incurring no debt.*

○ *A ramen profitable individual or company is making just enough money to cover basic living expenses.*

rate of re|turn (ABBR **ROR**) /reɪt əv rɪtɜrn/ (**rates of return**)

INVESTMENT

NOUN The **rate of return** of an investment is the amount of profit that it makes.

○ *High rates of return can be earned on these investments.*

○ *While there are no fixed rates of return, the yields on these units broadly reflect the interest rates prevailing in the market.*

real prop|er|ty /ril prɒpərti/

GENERAL

NOUN **Real property** is land, buildings, and anything attached to the land.

○ *Not only is your house real property, but so is the light fitting that hangs from the ceiling.*

○ *Real property is land and objects attached to land in a relatively permanent manner.*

r

re|ces|sion /rɪsɛʃ°n/ (recessions)

ECONOMICS

NOUN A **recession** is a decline in economic activity that lasts for two quarters or a year.

○ Countries with the lowest debt, and holding the most foreign debt, with the best labor force, will be the ones to emerge out of the global recession the fastest.

○ A worldwide financial panic was followed by the most serious recession since the Great Depression.

> **TALKING ABOUT RECESSIONS**
>
> A **deep** recession is very bad, while a **mild** recession is not too bad.
>
> If a recession gets worse, it **deepens** or **worsens**.
>
> If a company gets through a recession, it **weathers** or **survives** it.
>
> Something that causes a recession **triggers** it, and something that stops it happening **averts** or **avoids** it.
>
> A **double-dip** recession is one that starts to recover and then gets worse again before finally recovering.

re|deem /rɪdiːm/ (redeems, redeemed, redeeming)

INVESTMENT

VERB If you **redeem** a bond or mutual fund shares, you get the principal or cash back from it.

○ Bonds usually have a defined term, or maturity, after which the bond is redeemed, whereas stocks may be outstanding indefinitely.

○ A senior security is a security that, in the event of bankruptcy, will be redeemed before any other securities.

▶ **COLLOCATIONS:**
redeem a bond
redeem a security
redeem shares

red|lin|ing /rɛdlaɪnɪŋ/

MORTGAGE

NOUN **Redlining** is the bank practice of not lending in poor or minority areas.

○ *The law was enacted in response to both intentional redlining and structural barriers to credit for low-income communities.*

○ *A US federal law requires banks and thrifts to offer credit throughout their entire market area and prohibits them from redlining.*

re|fi|nance /rifaɪnæns/ (**refinances, refinanced, refinancing**)

MORTGAGE

VERB If a borrower **refinances** an existing loan, they find a lender who will replace it with a new loan with different terms.

○ *The bank comes under regulatory pressure to get the loans off the books, either by forcing borrowers to refinance them elsewhere or by foreclosing and selling the collateral.*

○ *Refinancing rental property when the real estate market is up requires patience from investors.*

> **WORD BUILDER**
> **re-** = again
>
> The prefix **re-** often appears in words that relate to doing something again: **debt restructuring**, **refinance**.

r

re|serve /rɪzɜrv/ (**reserves**)

BANKING

NOUN **Reserve** is the amount of money banks must have available to cover deposits.

○ *Legal reserve is the amount of money a bank or insurance company must keep to cover future claims and losses.*

○ *If you ensure that financial institutions have access to short-term credit, you encourage them to make loans rather than hoard reserves.*

re|sid|u|al /rɪzɪdʒuəl/

GENERAL

ADJECTIVE A **residual** amount is an amount that is left over or remains.

○ The total depreciation to be charged over the useful life will be the difference
between acquisition cost and residual value at the end of the asset's useful life.

○ Residual income is the operating income that an investment center earns
above a minimum desired return on invested assets.

▶ COLLOCATIONS:
residual amount
residual income
residual value

re|tained earn|ings /rɪteɪnd ɜrnɪŋz/

CORPORATE

NOUN **Retained earnings** are the profit that a company does not pay
out in dividends, but keeps in order to reinvest in itself.

○ Dividends and retained earnings come from after-tax income.

○ Most investment is financed within individual economic units – as when a
company pays for new plant from retained earnings.

ret|ro|ac|tive /rɛtrouæktɪv/

GENERAL

ADJECTIVE A **retroactive** transaction applies a change to previous
accounting periods.

○ There will be no retroactive adjustments in sales charges on investments
previously made during the 13-month period.

○ Disclosure must be provided of any retroactive change to prior period financial
statements, including the effect of any such change on income and income
per share.

▶ COLLOCATIONS:
retroactive adjustment
retroactive change
retroactive modification
retroactive restatement
retroactive revision

re|turn of cap|i|tal (ABBR **ROC**) /rɪtɜːn əv kæpɪtᵊl/

INVESTMENT

NOUN A **return of capital** is a situation in which you receive back money that was previously invested.

○ The company may be permitted to pay a liquidating dividend, and, because such payments are regarded as a return of capital, they are not taxed as income.

○ Dividends paid shortly after the purchase of shares by an investor, although in effect a return of capital, are taxable to shareholders who are subject to tax.

re|turn on as|sets (ABBR **ROA**) /rɪtɜːn ɒn æsɛts/

INVESTMENT

NOUN A **return on assets** is a measure of profitability that is calculated by dividing net income after interest and taxes by average total assets.

○ All firms would like to earn a higher return on assets, but their ability to do so is limited by competition.

○ In the US, the pharmaceutical sector has consistently generated the highest return on assets for the past two decades.

re|turn on cap|i|tal (ABBR **ROC**) /rɪtɜːn ɒn kæpɪtᵊl/

INVESTMENT

NOUN A **return on capital** is any earnings that you receive from the capital that you have invested.

○ As the total sales value is only 1.5 times the capital invested, the return on capital only works out at 15 percent.

○ The companies have greatly increased their return on capital as they have shed unproductive workers and subsidiaries or moved to low-cost locations.

re|turn on eq|ui|ty (ABBR **ROE**) /rɪtɜːn ɒn ɛkwɪti/

INVESTMENT

NOUN A **return on equity** is a measure of profitability that is calculated by dividing net income after interest and taxes by average common stockholders' equity.

○ The return on equity measures how well the owners are doing on their investment.

○ The company's treasury department actively takes risks in order to generate the return on equity demanded by investors.

re|turn on in|vest|ment (ABBR **ROI**) /rɪtɜrn ɒn ɪnvɛstmənt/
INVESTMENT

NOUN A **return on investment** is a measure of profitability that is calculated by dividing net profit by total assets.

○ *Incentive plans are usually based on indicators of corporate performance, such as net income, total dividends paid, or some specific return on investment.*

○ *However large the potential return on investment, companies will find it hard to raise money for new plants.*

rev|e|nue stream /rɛvənyu strim/ (**revenue streams**)
CORPORATE

NOUN A company's **revenue stream** is the money that it receives from selling a particular product or service.

○ *The events business was crucial to the group in that it provided a constant revenue stream.*

○ *A majority of the Fund's assets are in revenue bonds, which are backed by the revenue stream of a particular project.*

re|verse mort|gage /rɪvɜrs mɔrgɪdʒ/ (**reverse mortgages**)
MORTGAGE

NOUN A **reverse mortgage** is a mortgage on a paid-off property that provides money to an older retired person, to be paid back when the property is sold or when the person dies.

○ *A reverse mortgage enables the elderly, or certain others, to remain in their homes when they lack the income to pay for the upkeep cost of a house.*

○ *A reverse mortgage is used by older homeowners to receive income from the equity in their home to be repaid when they no longer occupy the home.*

Roth I|R|A /rɔθ aɪ ɑr eɪ/ (short for **Roth individual retirement account**) (**Roth IRAs**)
INVESTMENT: RETIREMENT

NOUN A **Roth IRA** is a kind of retirement account where contributions are made with taxed money, and distributions are tax-free. This retirement account is named for senator William Roth who sponsored the legislation to introduce it.

○ *A Roth IRA allows contributors to invest up to $2,000 per year, and to withdraw the principal and earnings totally tax-free under certain conditions.*

○ *A Roth IRA is designed to help you save for retirement, allowing after-tax contributions in exchange for the potential for tax-free income in retirement.*

R|S|U /ɑr ɛs yu/ (short for **restricted stock unit**)

INVESTMENT: STOCKS

ABBREVIATION An **RSU** is a grant valued in terms of company stock that takes the form of a promise that employees will receive stock in the future either as shares or the cash equivalent.

○ *An RSU is a share of stock that can't be sold or exchanged until it is vested.*

○ *Some RSU plans allow the employee to decide within certain limits exactly when he or she would like to receive the shares.*

R|T|G|S /ɑr ti dʒi ɛs/ (short for **real time gross settlement**)

BANKING

ABBREVIATION An **RTGS** is a type of electronic transfer where the money is immediately taken from the payer and the payee has access to it right away.

○ *The construction of the RTGS system permits large value transfers to clear and settle with immediate finality.*

○ *An RTGS system has been implemented, allowing for both real time and end-of-day delivery versus payment service.*

R|T|N /ɑr ti ɛn/ (short for **routing transit number**)

BANKING

ABBREVIATION An **RTN** is the code that identifies a financial institution on a check or transfer.

○ *RTNs are used in the electronic processing of checks.*

○ *A bank RTN identifies the bank a check is drawn on.*

run on a bank /rʌn ɒn ə bæŋk/

BANKING

PHRASE A **run on a bank** is a situation in which borrowers are worried that the bank will fail and they all try to withdraw money at the same time.

○ Central banks usually guarantee the deposits at commercial banks, and act as lender of last resort when there is a run on a bank.

○ Unless there's a run on a bank, most of the depositors won't show up at the same time for their money.

R

Ss

safe de|pos|it box /seɪf dɪpɒzɪt bɒks/ (**safe deposit boxes**)

BANKING

NOUN A **safe deposit box** is a small container stored in a bank vault that people can rent to keep valuables in.

○ Financial planners recommend storing hard-to-replace documents in a safe deposit box away from your home.

○ For example, if a burglar breaks into a safe deposit box and steals some securities and jewelry, the loss is covered.

sales rev|e|nue /seɪlz rɛvənyu/

CORPORATE

NOUN **Sales revenue** is money that a company or organization receives from sales of its goods and services.

○ They estimate that sales revenue will rise to $134 million.

○ A company generates sales revenue as a result of operating activities, which involve the sale of goods or services to customers.

Sal|lie Mae /sæli meɪ/ (short for **Student Loan Marketing Association**)

GENERAL

NOUN **Sallie Mae** is a publicly traded company that provides and trades in student loans.

○ Sallie Mae, the largest student loan provider, has just announced that it will charge fees for loan applications.

○ Sallie Mae, America's leading provider of education loans, owns or manages approximately $100 billion in student loans for more than seven million borrowers.

sav|ings ac|count /sˈeɪvɪŋz əkaʊnt/ (**savings accounts**)

BANKING

NOUN A **savings account** is a bank account with a limited number of transactions per month that pays a higher interest rate than a checking account.

○ *Balances above a certain amount in a checking account are automatically transferred into a savings account that pays interest.*

○ *An emergency fund is money set aside in a savings account to cover several months' living expenses.*

sav|ings and loan /sˈeɪvɪŋz ənd loʊn/ (**savings and loans**)

BANKING

NOUN A **savings and loan** is a financial institution that takes savings deposits and makes mortgage loans.

○ *Mortgage-backed bond prices also rose even though the nation's savings and loan associations continued to liquidate large amounts of the securities.*

○ *The savings and loan industry is the leading source of institutional finance for residential home mortgages in America.*

S cor|po|ra|tion /ɛs kɔrpəreɪʃᵊn/ (**S corporations**)

CORPORATE

NOUN An **S corporation** is a type of corporation in which the owners are taxed for any taxable income on their individual returns.

○ *Dealings in its own stock are not taxable to the S corporation.*

○ *If a corporation qualifies and chooses to become an S corporation, its income usually will be taxed to the shareholders.*

S|E|C /ɛs i si/ (short for **Securities and Exchange Commission**)

INVESTMENT: STOCKS

ABBREVIATION The **SEC** is the US agency responsible for regulating the financial reporting of companies whose stock is publicly traded.

○ *Private placement of securities directly to an institutional investor like an insurance company avoid the need for SEC registration if the securities are purchased for investment as opposed to resale.*

○ Filing with the SEC is required prior to selling restricted and control stock, and the number of shares that may be sold is limited.

---

se|cured /sɪkyʊərd/

BANKING

ADJECTIVE A **secured** loan or creditor has an asset such as a car or house pledged as collateral, that may be taken to satisfy the debt if the loan is not repaid.

○ Loans with collateral requirements are often referred to as secured loans.

○ Secured creditors take less risk because the credit that they extend is usually backed by collateral, such as a mortgage or other assets of the company.

---

se|cu|ri|ties /sɪkyʊərɪtiz/

INVESTMENT

NOUN **Securities** are financial or investment instruments that are bought and sold.

○ In a short sale, an investor sells borrowed securities, hoping to profit by buying them back later at a cheaper price.

○ Treasury notes are coupon-bearing securities, issued with 10 or fewer years to maturity.

---

seed cap|i|tal /siːd kæpɪtᵊl/

INVESTMENT: VENTURE CAPITALISM

NOUN **Seed capital** is an amount of money that a new company needs to pay for the costs of producing a business plan so that they can raise further capital to develop the company.

○ They are negotiating with financiers to raise seed capital for their latest venture.

○ Seed capital is provided to develop a concept, create the initial product, and carry out the first marketing efforts.

---

seed mon|ey /siːd mʌni/

INVESTMENT: VENTURE CAPITALISM

NOUN **Seed money** is money that is given to someone to help them start a new business or project.

○ *The government will give seed money to the project.*

○ *His former employer provided $1 million in seed money to develop the idea.*

---

sei|gnior|age /seɪnyərɪdʒ/

ECONOMICS

NOUN **Seigniorage** is the profit that a government makes by issuing money, because the value of the money is more than what it costs to produce the coins or bills.

○ *Seigniorage is the profit from making money and depends on the ability to have people hold your currency or other assets at a noncompetitive yield.*

○ *The US government earned about $6.3 billion in seigniorage from issuing collectible state quarters.*

---

sell|off /sɛlɔf/ (**selloffs**)

INVESTMENT: STOCKS

NOUN A **selloff** is a situation in which many investors sell their shares of a stock suddenly, often because of bad news.

○ *Friday saw the biggest one-day selloff of bonds since January as prices of the benchmark 30-year Treasury bond fell more than two points.*

○ *We are seeing a global selloff in government bonds, motivated by asset allocators.*

---

sell short /sɛl ʃɔrt/

INVESTMENT: STOCKS

PHRASE To **sell short** is to bet that a stock's price will go down by buying it now for a future price.

○ *Usually, investors sell short to profit from price declines.*

○ *Sometimes people will sell short a stock they already own in order to protect a paper profit.*

---

se|ri|al bonds /sɪəriəl bɒndz/

INVESTMENT: STOCKS

NOUN **Serial bonds** are bonds that are issued at the same time but have staggered maturity dates.

○ *The city will offer $729 million of tax-exempt bonds tentatively structured as serial bonds maturing in 2013 to 2020.*

○ *Serial bonds provide for the repayment of principal in a series of periodic installments.*

---

set|tle /sɛtᵊl/ (settles, settled, settling)

INVESTMENT: STOCKS

VERB If you **settle** a trade or security, you pay for and deliver securities that were traded.

○ *There is an obligation in the brokerage business to settle securities trades by the third day following the trade date.*

○ *Eurodollars are most commonly used to settle international transactions outside the United States.*

---

set|tle|ment a|gent /sɛtᵊlmənt eɪdʒənt/ (settlement agents)

INVESTMENT: STOCKS

NOUN A **settlement agent** is a person who arranges the transfer of securities or real property in a sale.

○ *Your settlement agent uses a closing statement to itemize all of the costs you and the seller will have to pay at closing to complete a real estate sale.*

○ *The escrow money was held by the settlement agent.*

---

set|tle|ment date /sɛtᵊlmənt deɪt/ (settlement dates)

INVESTMENT: STOCKS

NOUN A **settlement date** is the date on which a buyer pays for securities delivered by a seller, or the date on which title to real property passes from a seller to a buyer.

○ *The settlement date usually follows the trade date by five business days, but varies depending on the transaction and method of delivery used.*

○ *The contract outlines the payment schedule on the settlement date.*

S

set|tle|ment price /sɛtᵊlmənt praɪs/ (**settlement prices**)

INVESTMENT: STOCKS

NOUN The **settlement price** is the average price of a financial instrument at the end of a trading day.

○ *As futures markets have moved to round-the-clock trading, additional issues arise in determining a reasonable settlement price.*

○ *The settlement price is a value calculated according to a formula that varies from exchange to exchange.*

share /ʃɛər/ (**shares**)

INVESTMENT: STOCKS

NOUN A **share** is one of the equal parts that the value of a company is divided into and that you can buy as an investment.

○ *I've bought shares in my brother's new company.*

○ *People in China are eager to buy shares in new businesses.*

TALKING ABOUT SHARES

If their value goes up, shares **climb**, **jump**, **rise**, or **soar**. If their value goes down, shares **fall**, **plunge**, **tumble**, **slip**, or **slump**.

At the end of the day, people say that shares **close at** a particular price.

When a company **issues** shares, it makes them available to buy. People **trade** shares when they buy and sell them. If you **hold** shares **in** a company, you own some of its shares.

---

share cap|i|tal /ʃɛər kæpɪtᵊl/

INVESTMENT: STOCKS

NOUN **Share capital** is the maximum value of shares that a company can issue.

○ *A limited company is a company whose shareholders' maximum liability is limited to their share capital in the event of winding up.*

○ *Going public is used to indicate that a certain business is going to issue publicly traded share capital.*

share cer|tif|i|cate /ʃɛər sərtɪfɪkɪt/ (**share certificates**)

INVESTMENT: STOCKS

NOUN A **share certificate** is a document showing ownership of shares in a corporation.

○ *Global Registered Shares are the ordinary shares of a non-US company which trade both in the home market and the US with the same share certificate.*

○ *A share certificate is a written document that is signed on behalf of a corporation to serve as a legal proof of ownership of number of shares.*

▶ **SYNONYM:**
stock certificate

---

share|hold|er /ʃɛərhoʊldər/ (**shareholders**)

INVESTMENT: STOCKS

NOUN A **shareholder** is an investor who owns one or more shares of stock in a company.

○ *Under the plan, shareholders will exchange their common stock for an equal number of shares in the new holding company.*

○ *From the proceeds, the company said it will declare a distribution of $7.50 a share to its shareholders.*

> **WORD BUILDER**
> **-er** = person that does something
>
> The suffix **-er** often appears in words for people or organizations that do a particular thing: **backer**, **bondholder**, **dealer**, **fund manager**, **shareholder**.

S

---

share|hold|ers' eq|ui|ty /ʃɛərhoʊldərz ɛkwɪti/

INVESTMENT: STOCKS

NOUN **Shareholders' equity** is the total amount of ownership investment in a company.

○ *Shareholders' equity is comprised of all capital contributed to the entity including paid-in capital and retained earnings.*

○ *Paying dividends reduces shareholders' equity.*

share re|pur|chase /ʃɛər rɪpɜrtʃɪs/ (**share repurchases**)

INVESTMENT: STOCKS

NOUN A **share repurchase** is a situation in which a company buys back its own shares.

- ○ This year, our share repurchase activity will be down substantially from last year because we are using our cash to fund the new acquisition.

- ○ Since our first share repurchase program began, we have repurchased $2.8 billion worth of stock.

▶ **SYNONYM:**
  stock buyback

---

sink|ing fund /sɪŋkɪŋ fʌnd/ (**sinking funds**)

CORPORATE

NOUN A **sinking fund** is a fund where a company sets aside money for future repayment of bonds.

- ○ Cash flows received by the trust in excess of the sinking fund requirement are also allocated to other bond classes.

- ○ The remaining funds would be put into a sinking fund which constituted a trust fund.

---

small-cap /smɔl kæp/

INVESTMENT: STOCKS

ADJECTIVE A **small-cap** company or stock is a company or stock that is worth under $1 billion.

- ○ Almost half of the stocks in our portfolio have market caps of less than $1 billion; these small-cap investments currently account for about one-fourth of net assets.

- ○ This fund's objective is to seek long-term capital appreciation by investing primarily in securities of small-cap companies.

---

soft cur|ren|cy /sɔft kɜrənsi/ (**soft currencies**)

FOREIGN EXCHANGE

NOUN A **soft currency** is a fluctuating currency from an economically or politically unstable country that is not widely accepted in other countries.

○ *A true soft currency can't be exchanged on the open market (but quite possibly can be exchanged on the black market for hard currency).*

○ *A soft currency is expected to fluctuate erratically or depreciate against other currencies.*

---

sov|er|eign debt /sɒvərɪn dɛt/

ECONOMICS

NOUN **Sovereign debt** is government debt in a currency other than a government's own national currency.

○ *The Eurozone crisis could be resolved simply by pushing the button on the purchase of Eurozone sovereign debt in sufficient quantities to stabilize financial markets.*

○ *The excessive levels of sovereign debt will slow economic growth to zero or below.*

SOX /sɒks/ (short for **Sarbanes-Oxley Act**)

INVESTMENT: STOCKS

ABBREVIATION **SOX** is an act that was passed by the US congress in 2002 to protect investors from fraudulent accounting by businesses.

○ *With the passage of SOX, the costs of reporting and governance that are associated with being a public firm grew significantly.*

○ *Since privately held firms are not heavily regulated by regulations such as SOX, they have greater operational flexibility.*

---

spec|u|la|tion /spɛkyəleɪʃⁿn/

INVESTMENT

NOUN **Speculation** is the act of making very risky investments in the hope of large gains.

○ *Internet companies with little to no profits were going public and enjoying significant stock price increases often based solely on industry speculation.*

○ *The Euro ended speculation among the different national currencies.*

---

spin off /spɪn ɒf/ (**spins off, spun off, spinning off**)

CORPORATE

VERB If you **spin off** a company or subsidiary, you sell a subsidiary part of a company, or make a subsidiary its own separate company by issuing shares in the new company.

○ *A common technique for spinning off a company from its parent is to distribute shares in the new company to the old company's shareholders.*

○ *The company intends to spin off its regional operating companies to investors.*

---

spot mar|ket /spɒt mɑrkɪt/ (**spot markets**)

INVESTMENT

NOUN A **spot market** is when investors are selling securities or commodities for cash at the current time.

○ *When a commodity is traded in the spot market, goods are sold for cash and delivered immediately.*

○ *Starbucks bought futures contracts for coffee to avoid the volatility of the spot market.*

---

spot price /spɒt praɪs/ (**spot prices**)

INVESTMENT

NOUN A **spot price** is a cash price for securities or commodities for immediate delivery.

○ *Par is the term applied when the forward price of the purchase or sale of a currency is the same as the spot price.*

○ *The spot price of gold has been rising due to fear of inflation.*

---

spot rate /spɒt reɪt/ (**spot rates**)

FOREIGN EXCHANGE

NOUN The **spot rate** is the exchange rate for a currency at the current time.

○ *Bank notes are normally priced at a premium to the current spot rate for a currency.*

○ *If foreign currency markets are efficient, the forward rate should reflect what market participants expect the future spot rate for a currency to be.*

---

spread /sprɛd/ (**spreads**)

INVESTMENT

NOUN The **spread** of a financial instrument is the difference between the selling price and the purchase price.

○ *If a seller narrows the spread, they reduce the difference between the bid and ask prices of a security.*

○ *The size of the spread from one asset to another will differ mainly because of the difference in liquidity of each asset.*

---

stalk|ing horse /stɔkɪŋ hɔrs/ (stalking horses)

INVESTMENT

NOUN A **stalking horse** is a buyer who has agreed to make a minimum bid before a bankruptcy auction.

○ *The sale process will now be conducted without a stalking horse bid.*

○ *The stalking horse bidder typically enters into a sale contract with the debtor for the subject assets, thereby setting a floor, or minimum bid.*

---

stand|ing set|tle|ment in|struc|tions /stændɪŋ sɛtəlmənt ɪnstrʌkʃənz/

INVESTMENT

NOUN **Standing settlement instructions** are instructions that have been agreed in advance, and that are to be used every time a trade is made.

○ *For recurring transfer of funds or securities, you may enter standing settlement instructions that can be used each time a transfer request is made.*

○ *Standing settlement instructions improve efficiency by creating consistent settlement instructions for all your deals.*

---

start|up /stɑrtʌp/ (startups)

INVESTMENT: VENTURE CAPITALISM

NOUN A **startup** is a new company that is just beginning operations.

○ *The firm invests funds in startups, and encourages technologies and first-time ideas.*

○ *A startup company will often have the search for funding as the primary focus of its business plan.*

S

state|ment of cash flows /ˈsteɪtmənt əv kæʃ floʊz/
(**statements of cash flows**)

CORPORATE

NOUN A **statement of cash flows** is a financial statement that shows the amounts of cash that came into and went out of a company over a particular period of time.

○ *By using a statement of cash flows, managers can plan and manage their cash sources and needs from different types of business activities.*

○ *Whatever the sources and uses of cash, the statement of cash flows tells a great deal about a business's health.*

state|ment of earn|ings and com|pre|hen|sive in|come /ˈsteɪtmənt əv ˈɜrnɪŋz ənd kɒmprɪˈhɛnsɪv ˈɪnkʌm/
(**statements of earnings and comprehensive income**)

CORPORATE

NOUN A **statement of earnings and comprehensive income** is a single financial statement that contains all items of income and expense for a particular accounting period.

○ *The Financial Accounting Standards Board requires a single statement of earnings and comprehensive income and requires a subtotal for net income.*

○ *The regulations require a single combined statement of earnings and comprehensive income rather than separate earnings and income statements.*

stock¹ /stɒk/ (**stocks**)

INVESTMENT: STOCKS

NOUN A **stock** is one of the parts or shares that the value of a company is divided into, that people can buy.

○ *She works for a bank, buying and selling stocks.*

○ *Investors bought stock in the new computer company.*

stock² /stɒk/

INVESTMENT: STOCKS

NOUN A company's **stock** is the total number of its shares.

○ *Two years later, when the company went public, their stock was valued at $38 million.*

○ *The parent company owns 90 percent of the subsidiary company's outstanding common stock.*

---

stock div|i|dend /stɒk dɪvɪdɛnd/ (**stock dividends**)

INVESTMENT: STOCKS

NOUN A **stock dividend** is a dividend payment that is made with additional shares of stock instead of cash.

○ *The stock dividend may be additional shares in the company, or it may be shares in a subsidiary being spun off to shareholders.*

○ *If the company declares a stock dividend, we will credit your account with the appropriate number of shares on the payment date.*

---

stock op|tions /stɒk ɒpʃᵊnz/

INVESTMENT: STOCKS

NOUN **Stock options** are the right to buy a stock in the future at a price set today.

○ *The basic per share amount does not take into consideration the possible effects of stock options, which would increase the number of shares outstanding.*

○ *He believes in providing stock options to his best employees.*

---

stock split /stɒk splɪt/ (**stock splits**)

INVESTMENT: STOCKS

NOUN A **stock split** is a situation in which the number of shares outstanding by a company is increased, usually to make the price of shares lower.

○ *A stock split increases the total number of shares while lowering the price of each share without changing the market capitalization, or total value, of the shares held.*

○ *If a management team believes the shares of its firm are undervalued, it can signal this to potential investors by performing a stock split.*

S

stock sym|bol /stɒk sɪmbᵊl/ (stock symbols)

INVESTMENT: STOCKS

NOUN A **stock symbol** is a standard abbreviation for a publicly traded stock.

○ Ticker tape is a computerized device that relays to investors around the world the stock symbol and the latest price and volume on securities as they are traded.

○ A stock symbol may represent a single company or any number of different security offerings issued by a company.

▶ SYNONYM:
ticker symbol

stock war|rant /stɒk wɔrənt/ (stock warrants)

INVESTMENT: STOCKS

NOUN A **stock warrant** is the right to buy stock at a particular price on a particular date directly from the issuing company.

○ Attached to each bond was one detachable stock warrant entitling the holder to purchase 10 shares of the company's common stock.

○ If the company issues a stock warrant, they enter into a contract to buy or sell stocks from the investors.

stop pay|ment /stɒp peɪmənt/

BANKING

PHRASE If a bank **stops payment**, it cancels payment in progress on a check on the payer's instructions.

○ If you do not want a check you wrote to be cashed, you can instruct your bank to stop payment.

○ Bank fees for stopping payment on a check can be $30 to $50.

strad|dle /strædᵊl/ (straddles)

INVESTMENT

NOUN A **straddle** is the act of purchasing both call and put options for the same investment.

S

○ A straddle involves the purchase or sale of an equal number of puts and calls with the same terms at the same time.

○ Where the investor expects a sharp movement in the share price, but is unsure of the direction it will take, the long straddle may be appropriate.

---

strike price /straɪk praɪs/ (strike prices)

INVESTMENT: STOCKS

NOUN The **strike price** is the price of an option when it is exercised.

○ Often the number of shares available to be exercised at the strike price will increase as time passes.

○ Strike price plays a crucial role in both the value of the option and the potential for profit.

---

sub|or|di|nat|ed /səbɔrdᵊneɪtɪd/

MORTGAGE

ADJECTIVE A **subordinated** loan is a loan that has less legal priority to be repaid.

○ In the event of bankruptcy, senior debt must be repaid before subordinated debt is repaid.

○ In the event of bankruptcy, subordinated debtholders receive payment only after senior debt claims are paid in full.

> **WORD BUILDER**
> **sub-** = less important, or a smaller part
>
> The prefix **sub-** often appears in words connected with something that is a smaller part of another thing, or with words to do with passing on a responsibility, debt, etc. to someone else: **subordinated**, **subprime**, **subsidiary**.

---

sub|prime loan /sʌbpraɪm loʊn/ (subprime loans)

MORTGAGE

NOUN A **subprime loan** is a loan with a higher interest rate, to borrowers who are a high credit risk.

○ *Loans of lower initial credit quality, which are more likely to experience significantly higher levels of default, are classified as subprime loans.*

○ *Subprime loans are made at a higher interest rate than most other loans to borrowers who do not qualify for ordinary loans because of bad credit rating.*

---

sub|sid|i|ar|y /səbsɪdiɛri/ (subsidiaries)

CORPORATE

NOUN A **subsidiary** is a company that is part of a larger and more important company.

○ *WM Financial Services is a subsidiary of Washington Mutual.*

○ *They are considering raising part of their future capital requirements by forming new subsidiaries and selling a portion of their equity to the public.*

---

sunk cost /sʌŋk kɔst/ (sunk costs)

ECONOMICS

NOUN A **sunk cost** is an expense that you have already paid for or committed to and which you cannot change.

○ *The sunk cost is the money that cannot be recovered by subsequent resale of an asset.*

○ *A sunk cost is money, time, or another resource that has been irretrievably spent.*

---

sur|ren|der /sərɛndər/ (surrenders, surrendered, surrendering)

INVESTMENT

VERB If you **surrender** an investment such as an insurance policy, you cash it out before maturity at a penalty.

○ *The insurer pays the insured the cash value which the policy has built up if it is surrendered.*

○ *Both companies' stocks are surrendered and new company stock is issued in its place.*

swap /swɒp/ (swaps)

INVESTMENT

NOUN A **swap** is the exchange of one security or investment for another.

○ *The buyer of a swaption has the right to enter into an interest rate swap agreement by some specified date in the future.*

○ *Swap contracts generally do not involve exchanges of principal.*

swap|tion /swɒpʃən/ (swaptions)

INVESTMENT

NOUN A **swaption** is an over-the-counter option on a swap.

○ *The buyer of a swaption has the right to enter into an interest rate swap agreement by some specified date in the future.*

○ *The government refused retrospectively to legalize interest-rate swaps and swaptions entered into during the 1980s.*

sweat eq|ui|ty /swɛt ɛkwɪti/

INVESTMENT: VENTURE CAPITALISM

NOUN **Sweat equity** is the ownership of a share of equity in a startup by working rather than investing money.

○ *Employees can receive sweat equity for work performed on an asset to increase the value through improvements.*

○ *The engineer contributed sweat equity instead of capital to earn his share of the company's stock.*

SWIFT /swɪft/ (short for **Society for Worldwide Interbank Financial Telecommunication**)

BANKING

ABBREVIATION **SWIFT** is an organization that supplies secure messaging services and software to financial institutions.

○ *SWIFT is a dedicated computer network to support funds transfer messages internationally between over 900 member banks worldwide.*

○ *SWIFT is an international consortium of member banks operating a worldwide system for transfer of money and messages.*

S

Tt

---

tax ha|ven /tæks heɪvᵊn/ (tax havens)

Tax

NOUN A **tax haven** is a country or place that has a low rate of tax so that people choose to live there or register companies there in order to avoid paying higher tax in their own countries.

○ *The Caribbean has become an important location for international banking because it is a tax haven.*

○ *A tax haven is a foreign country or corporation used to avoid or reduce income taxes, especially by investors from another country.*

---

tax hol|i|day /tæks hɒlɪdeɪ/ (tax holidays)

Tax

NOUN A **tax holiday** is a period during which a person or company is allowed to pay no tax or less tax than usual.

○ *There is a five-year tax holiday for new power plants.*

○ *A five-year tax holiday for new power plants brought in a $1 billion project by foreign investors.*

---

tax shel|ter /tæks ʃɛltər/ (tax shelters)

Tax

NOUN A **tax shelter** is a way of arranging the finances of a business or a person so that they have to pay less tax.

○ *Losses on a sale of stock may not be used as tax shelter if equivalent stock is purchased 30 days or less before or after the sale of the stock.*

○ *The tax shelter encouraged investors to band together in syndicates that would commission new freighters.*

T-bill /tiː bɪl/ (short for **Treasury bill**) (**T-bills**)

INVESTMENT

NOUN A **T-bill** is a government issued security with a maturity of one year or less.

○ When you purchase a T-bill, you do not receive interest in the form of a coupon; instead it is sold at a discount from par.

○ Part of the increase in interest rates can be attributed to pressures on the 91-day T-bill rate, which serves as a benchmark for commercial paper transactions.

T-bond /tiː bɒnd/ (short for **Treasury bond**) (**T-bonds**)

INVESTMENT

NOUN A **T-bond** is a government issued security with a maturity of more than 10 years.

○ The futures price quoted is based on the underlying T-bond price with 8 percent coupon and 20-year maturity.

○ T-bonds pay interest with coupons twice a year.

teas|er rate /tiːzər reɪt/ (**teaser rates**)

BANKING: CREDIT

NOUN A **teaser rate** is a low introductory interest rate on credit that goes up after a short time.

○ With adjustable rate mortgages, the interest rate is not fixed – there is a 2 year teaser rate, and then interest goes up for the next 20 years.

○ The teaser rate to attract investors was 1.5%, going up to 6% after a year.

ten|der of|fer /tɛndər ɔfər/ (**tender offers**)

INVESTMENT

NOUN A **tender offer** is an offer to buy shares directly from shareholders at a higher than market price, that can be part of a takeover bid or a share repurchase.

○ A hostile takeover with the aim of replacing current existing management is usually attempted through a public tender offer.

○ The acquirer made a tender offer directly to shareholders of the target company to sell their shares.

t

term sheet /tɜrm ʃit/ (**term sheets**)

INVESTMENT: VENTURE CAPITALISM

NOUN A **term sheet** is a non-binding listing of preliminary terms for venture capital financing.

○ The venture capital investor will offer a term sheet offering to purchase shares at a price based on its estimate of the company's pre-money valuation.

○ We would require delivery of the term sheet before an investor makes a binding investment decision.

terms of pay|ment /tɜrmz əv peɪmənt/

GENERAL

NOUN The **terms of payment** of a sale state how and when an invoice is to be paid.

○ The terms of payment were 50 percent down and 50 percent on completion.

○ The leading auctioneers offer inducements such as guaranteed prices to persuade sellers to part with their treasures, and generous terms of payment for buyers.

tick|er /tɪkər/ (**tickers**)

INVESTMENT: STOCKS

NOUN A **ticker** is a list of the current prices of stocks, often scrolling across a screen.

○ You may not receive the same price that you noticed on the stock ticker if too much time has gone by or the stock made a sudden increase or decrease.

○ Monitoring a stock ticker is a great way to keep up with your investments and stay abreast of stock market activity with a quick glance.

time de|pos|it /taɪm dɪpɒzɪt/ (**time deposits**)

BANKING

NOUN A **time deposit** is money that has been placed in a bank account and cannot be withdrawn until a particular amount of time has passed.

○ If such additional early withdrawal penalties are not imposed, the account ceases to be a time deposit account.

○ A time deposit from which partial early withdrawals are permitted must impose additional early withdrawal penalties.

ti|tle /taɪtᵊl/

GENERAL

NOUN **Title** to property is legal written proof of ownership.

○ *Should the mortgagor fail to pay the mortgage within a specified period of time, the mortgage holder gains the title to the property with no obligation to sell it.*

○ *In a cooperative, the corporation or association owns title to the real estate.*

track|er /trækər/ (**trackers**)

INVESTMENT

NOUN A **tracker** is a fund that follows or tracks a market index.

○ *An index tracker fund is a collective investment vehicle that is designed to follow the performance of a particular index.*

○ *A tracker fund invests to try to emulate movement of the index.*

tranche /trɑnʃ/ (**tranches**)

MORTGAGE

NOUN A **tranche** is a portion of a type of financial instrument that is divided into risk classes.

○ *Each tranche offers a varying degree of risk and return so as to meet investor demand.*

○ *Investors in the most risky tranches receive the highest payouts, but are the first to lose their payments if loans in the pool default.*

trans|fer pric|ing /trænsfɜr praɪsɪŋ/

CORPORATE

NOUN **Transfer pricing** is the setting of a price for the transfer of materials, goods, or services between different parts of a large organization.

○ *He claims that foreign companies are engaged in massive tax avoidance through transfer pricing.*

○ *The foreign partner should resist transfer pricing of components at a higher-than-market price.*

t

trans|la|tion /trænzleɪʃⁿn/

FOREIGN EXCHANGE

NOUN **Translation** is the act of converting one currency into another.

○ *Revenues and earnings remain under pressure from the negative impact of translation of international currencies into a stronger US dollar.*

○ *Profits denominated in a foreign currency carry a translation risk.*

Treas|ur|y /trɛʒəri/

ECONOMICS

NOUN The **Treasury** is the US government department responsible for money, taxes, and revenue.

○ *It is the Treasury's job to issue currency and control the nation's credit.*

○ *The Treasury Department released details of the new corporate tax rates.*

treas|ur|y stock /trɛʒəri stɒk/

CORPORATE

NOUN **Treasury stock** is stock that has been bought back by the company that issued it.

○ *When the treasury stock is sold back on the open market, the paid-in capital is either debited or credited if it is sold for more or less than the initial cost respectively.*

○ *Treasury stock receives no dividends and does not carry voting power while held by the company.*

trust ac|count /trʌst əkaʊnt/ (**trust accounts**)

INVESTMENT

NOUN A **trust account** is an account that is held in trust for someone else, such as a minor or an estate.

○ *It may be illegal to take money out of a trust account and not use it for the benefit of the beneficiary.*

○ *The inheritance money will be held in a trust account for her until her 21st birthday.*

Uu

un|der|wa|ter /ˌʌndərwɔːtər/

ADJECTIVE An **underwater** loan is a loan where the collateral such as a house is worth less than the principal still owing.

- ○ *Banks always pursue you if you could pay the underwater part of the mortgage, especially if you have money in the bank.*
- ○ *Underwater homeowners whose mortgages exceed the value of their homes are encouraged to refinance at lower rates.*

un|der|write /ˌʌndərraɪt/ (underwrites, underwrote, underwritten, underwriting)

VERB If an investment bank **underwrites** securities, it manages the issuing of securities for a company.

- ○ *In underwriting, one or more securities firms or banks, forming a syndicate, buy an entire issue of bonds from an issuer and re-sell them to investors.*
- ○ *Facebook chose JP Morgan Chase to underwrite its IPO.*

u|nit trust /ˈyuːnɪt trʌst/ (unit trusts)

NOUN A **unit trust** is an investment fund that sells shares of a fixed portfolio of securities.

- ○ *The return on investment of unit holders is usually in the form of income distribution and capital appreciation, derived from the pool of assets supporting the unit trust fund.*
- ○ *A unit trust is a collective investment plan that pools the savings of a large number of investors.*

un|load /ʌnlǒud/ (unloads, unloaded, unloading)

INVESTMENT

VERB If you **unload** investments, you sell them.

○ *Since March, he has unloaded 1.3 million shares and bought 1.1 million.*

○ *In the two years that followed the NASDAQ fall, venture capitalists unloaded many of their investments at a loss.*

WORD BUILDER
un- = not

The prefix **un-** is often added to adjectives to make their opposites: **unload, unsecured**.

un|se|cured /ʌnsɪkyǔərd/

BANKING: CREDIT

ADJECTIVE An **unsecured** loan or debt is not guaranteed by an asset such as a person's home.

○ *The group's total debts include $900 million in unsecured loans and an additional $700 million that is secured against specific assets.*

○ *Two scandals involving local banks whose managements had lent millions of dollars in unsecured loans have sapped public confidence.*

U|S Sa|vings bond /yu ɛs sěɪvɪŋz bɒnd/ (US Savings bonds)

INVESTMENT

NOUN A **US Savings bond** is a long-term bond issued by the US government that is considered low-risk.

○ The Patriot bond is a form of US Savings bond issued after 9/11.

○ All US Savings bonds stop earning interest at final maturity, 40 years or less from issue.

---

u|su|ry /yu̱ʒəri/

ECONOMICS

NOUN **Usury** is excessive interest charges on a loan.

○ If the discount rate is 7.0 percent, then national banks may charge 8.0 percent, discounted in advance, without regard to state usury laws.

○ Most major credit card issuers are based in states without usury laws and can charge any interest rate they wish.

u

Vv

---

val|u|a|tion /ˈvælyueɪʃᵊn/ (valuations)

GENERAL

NOUN A **valuation** is a judgment that someone makes about how much something is worth.

- ○ The company said that the total purchase price is slightly below the low end of its valuation of these assets.
- ○ If the market valuation of the subsidiary does increase, the gains should, at a later date, spill over to the shareholder.

---

ven|ture cap|i|tal (ABBR **VC**) /ˈvɛntʃər kæpɪtᵊl/

INVESTMENT: VENTURE CAPITALISM

NOUN **Venture capital** is money that is invested in projects that have a high risk of failure, but that will bring large profits if they are successful.

- ○ It is widely believed that venture capital facilitates more innovative activities and is a critical aspect of national growth.
- ○ Venture capital firms can assist entrepreneurs with setting up their businesses.

---

ven|ture cap|i|tal|ist (ABBR **VC**) /ˈvɛntʃər kæpɪtᵊlɪst/ (venture capitalists)

INVESTMENT: VENTURE CAPITALISM

NOUN A **venture capitalist** is someone who makes money by investing in very risky projects.

- ○ Many venture capitalists are making investments in software and networking businesses.

○ In the usual model, the venture capitalist is involved in management and mentoring of the startup.

---

vest|ing /vɛstɪŋ/

INVESTMENT: STOCKS

NOUN **Vesting** is the situation in which an employee gains ownership of retirement funds or stock options after a period of time.

○ The vesting schedule indicates the length of time employees are required to remain with their employer before they earn the right to their stock options or retirement account balances.

○ A delay in absolute ownership of benefits is called vesting.

---

void /vɔɪd/ (**voids, voided, voiding**)

BANKING

VERB If you **void** a check or an invoice, you cancel it by changing the amount to zero, while leaving the transaction still posted.

○ Items that are sequentially numbered such as checks, invoices, and purchase orders are voided rather than deleted so that every numbered document can be accounted for.

○ When you void an invoice, the invoice number continues to exist so that you can account for it.

---

vos|tro ac|count /vɒstroʊ əkaʊnt/ (**vostro accounts**)

BANKING

NOUN A **vostro account** is an account that a domestic bank holds for another foreign bank in the domestic bank's currency. "Vostro" is from the Latin "voster," meaning "your."

○ A vostro account is maintained by a foreign bank in India with their corresponding bank.

○ In a vostro account, the administrators are not actually the owners of the money, but they must keep this account solvent on behalf of its owner.

V

vouch|er /ˈvaʊtʃər/ (**vouchers**)

GENERAL

NOUN A **voucher** is a document showing payment information, or a document that can be presented to receive money.

○ *The plan will give vouchers to cover the cost of private treatment if waiting lists are too long.*

○ *Cash welfare benefits were replaced with vouchers for food and other essentials.*

V

Ww

---

wash sale /wɒʃ seɪl/ (wash sales)

INVESTMENT: STOCKS

NOUN A **wash sale** is the act of selling a security at a loss and then buying the same security again shortly after.

- Wash sale rules restrict an investor from deducting the loss on a security if repurchased within 30 days.
- Day traders may buy and sell the same stock frequently which can result in a wash sale.

---

weight|ed av|er|age cost of cap|i|tal (ABBR WACC)
/weɪtɪd ævərɪdʒ kɒst əv kæpɪtᵊl/

INVESTMENT

NOUN The **weighted average cost of capital** is the cost of capital that is adjusted according to the percentages of debt financing and equity financing.

- The weighted average cost of capital takes into account both debt and equity sources of capital.
- Investors use the weighted average cost of capital to find good investment opportunities.

---

white knight /waɪt naɪt/ (white knights)

INVESTMENT

NOUN A **white knight** is a person or an organization that rescues a company from financial difficulties.

- They need to find a white knight to provide the $300m that the banks are demanding.

W

○ With the higher bid offered by the white knight, the predator might not remain interested in acquisition and hence the target company is protected from the raid.

---

wind|fall prof|its /wɪndfɔl prɒfɪts/

CORPORATE

NOUN **Windfall profits** are excessive profits with a non-business cause such as a natural disaster.

○ Following Hurricane Katrina, the US Congress was proposing to impose a windfall profits tax on the privately owned oil companies.

○ His spendthrift policies have all but depleted the country's reserves, which ought to be brimming with past windfall profits from oil and gas.

---

wire trans|fer /waɪər trænsfər/ (wire transfers)

BANKING

NOUN A **wire transfer** is a direct payment of money from one bank account into another.

○ The fastest but most expensive arrangement for transferring funds is wire transfer, and a slower but cheaper method is a depository transfer check.

○ Can you stop payment on an electronic wire transfer in the same way as you can with checks?

---

work|ing cap|i|tal /wɜrkɪŋ kæpɪtᵊl/

CORPORATE

NOUN **Working capital** is money available for use immediately, rather than money invested in land or equipment.

○ He borrowed a further $1.5m to provide working capital.

○ Less than 5 percent of the company's working capital requirements came from bank financing.

W

Yy

yield /yiːld/ (yields)

INVESTMENT

NOUN The **yield** of an investment is the amount of money or profit that it produces.

- The high yields available on the dividend shares made them attractive to private investors.

- Real estate prices are low, but the rental market is likely to produce better yields.

---

yield curve /yiːld kɜrv/ (yield curves)

ECONOMICS

NOUN A **yield curve** is a graph showing the interest rates of bonds that mature at different times.

- There is a negative yield curve when the yield on a short-term security is higher than the yield on a long-term security.

- A yield curve shows the interest rates on government debt of different maturities.

---

yield to ma|tur|i|ty (ABBR **YTM**) /yiːld tə mətyʊəriti/ (yields to maturity)

INVESTMENT

NOUN The **yield to maturity** of a bond is the rate of return on the bond if it is held to its maturity date.

- The yield to maturity on the bond is determined based on the bond's credit rating relative to a government security with similar maturity or duration.

- The yield to maturity on the active-issues index of the Wall Street brokerage fell below 19 percent.

y

Zz

ze|ro-cou|pon bonds /zɪərou kupɒn bɒndz/

INVESTMENT

NOUN **Zero-coupon bonds** are bonds with no coupons that do not pay interest, and are sold at a large discount from their face value.

- Governments keen to tap investor demand for their securities sometimes issue zero-coupon bonds.

- Zero-coupon bonds do not pay interest but can be redeemed at full face value at maturity.

Practice
and
Solutions

1. Find the words or phrases that do not belong.

1 Types of mortgage ....
   a balloon mortgage   **b** square mortgage   **c** conventional mortgage
   d reverse mortgage

2 Types of fund ....
   a fence fund   **b** mutual fund   **c** hedge fund   **d** sinking fund

3 Types of bank ....
   a commercial bank   **b** custodian bank   **c** hedge bank
   d correspondent bank

4 Types of loan ....
   a bridge loan   **b** payday loan   **c** closed-end loan   **d** custodian loan

5 Types of bonds ....
   a muni bonds   **b** balloon bonds   **c** junk bonds   **d** serial bonds

2. Complete the sentences by writing one word or phrase in each gap.

corporation	depreciation	valuation
maturity	annuity	liquid assets

1 Most people only ask for a .... when they
intend to sell.

2 She used her pension savings to buy an ....

3 Terminal bonuses will be paid when the policy reaches
....

4 He is the president of a large electronics ....

5 The company has enough .... to finance operations for three months.

6 The cost of maintenance and .... of the vehicles is carried by the owners.

3. Match the two parts together.

1 If a business or person breaks even,

    a you pay it back in regular payments.

2 If you float a company,

    b you cancel it by changing the amount to zero.

3 If you amortize a debt,

    c you buy a series of them that mature in sequence.

4 If you redeem a bond or mutual fund shares,

    d you sell shares in it to the public.

5 If you void a check or an invoice,

    e they earn as much money as they spend.

6 If you ladder investments,

    f you get the principal or cash back from it.

4. For each question, choose the correct answer.

a speculation   an allocation   a valuation

1 An amount of money that is given to a particular person or used for a particular purpose is ....

| a backwardation | a modification | a demutualization |

2 A situation in which a mutually owned company such as an insurance
   company changes into a public company that issues stock is
   ....

| speculation | translation | capitalization |

3 The act of making very risky investments in the hope of large gains is
   ....

| modification | speculation | diversification |

4 The act of investing in different industries, areas, countries, and types
   of financial instruments, to reduce the chance that all of the
   investments will drop in price at the same time is
   ....

| backwardation | loss on translation | speculation |

5 A situation in which the price of a forward or futures contract is trading
   below the expected spot price when the contract matures is
   ....

| translation | capitalization | amortization |

6 The sum of the total share capital issued by a company is its
   ....

5. Rearrange the letters to find words. Use the definitions to help you.

1 ssceernoi   ....
   (a decline in economic activity that lasts for two quarters or a year)

2 ergrem ....
(the joining together of two separate companies or organizations so
that they become one)

3 eraibrtga ....
(the simultaneous purchase and sale of an asset in order to take
advantage of a difference in price)

4 idenddiv ....
(an amount of a company's profits that is paid to people who own
shares in the company)

5 veelegar ....
(the amount of borrowed money that a company uses to run its business)

6 threnipraps ....
(a company that is owned by two or more people, who share in the
risks and rewards of the business)

6. Choose the correct word to fill each gap.

blue-chip	bolt-on	large-cap

1 A .... stock is a stock that has a long stable
history of earnings.

convertible	negotiable	subordinated

2 A .... loan is a loan that has less legal priority to
be repaid.

overlimit	residual	outstanding

3 Money that is .... has not yet been paid and is
still owed to someone.

Outstanding	Cumulative	Convertible

4 .... dividends or earnings are added on from period to period.

front-end	secured	pro forma

5 A company's .... balance or earnings are their expected balance or earnings.

Over-the-counter	Ex-dividend	Intangible

6 .... shares are not bought and sold on a stock exchange, but directly with a broker.

7. Put each sentence into the correct order.

1 in salaries / are not / increases / with inflation / keeping up

....

....

2 has announced / of five / its acquisition / local stores / the supermarket giant

....

....

3 profit margins / remain / on such / low cost items / extremely low

....

....

4 of stocks / selloff / the Federal Reserve / the recent / has worried

....

....

5 by the end of / we expect / to improve / the company's figures / the fiscal year

....

....

6 payday loans / high-interest / reliant on / workers are / many low-paid

....

....

8. Choose the correct word to fill each gap.

horse	warrior	knight

1 Someone making an unwelcome takeover attempt of a company is called a black ....

pill	dose	letter

2 A way of trying to stop a takeover by doing something to make the company worth much less if the takeover were successful is called a poison ....

bull	bear	cattle

3 A situation in which people are selling a lot of shares of stock because they expect the price to drop is called a .... market.

dog	bear	horse

4 A buyer who has agreed to make a minimum bid before a bankruptcy auction is called a stalking ....

PRACTICE PRACTICE PRACTICE PRACTICE PRACTICE

fishing scraping dealing

5 Investing in low-priced securities in the hope of making a profit is called
bottom ....

handshake parachute bonus

6 A very large payment and benefits that are offered to executives as part
of their employment agreement if they are forced to leave a company is
called a golden ....

9. Complete the sentences by writing one word in each gap.

tracker backer merger
ticker broker voucher

1 A .... is a commissioned agent who buys and
sells securities for investors.

2 A .... is a list of the current prices of stocks,
often scrolling across a screen.

3 A .... is a fund that follows or tracks a market
index.

4 A .... is a document showing payment
information, or a document that can be presented to receive money.

5 A .... is someone who helps or supports a
project, an organization, or a person, usually by giving money.

6 A .... is the joining together of two separate
companies or organizations so that they become one.

10. Match the two parts together.

1 The business needs to have enough working capital

   a unless it received a $15 million payment.

2 There may be a conflict of interest

   b extra finance was easy to secure.

3 The mortgage company threatened foreclosure

   c the base rate charged to customers of commercial banks.

4 All the shareholders lost the share capital

   d to meet its short-term debts.

5 An attractive rate of return meant that

   e they had invested in the business.

6 The interbank rate of interest influences

   f between bondholders and shareholders.

11. Which sentences are correct?

1 If someone files for bankruptcy, they avoid becoming bankrupt. ....

2 If someone exports commodities, they sell them to another country. ....

3 If an exchange rate is favorable, it gives you an advantage. ....

4 If something curbs inflation, it causes it to rise. ....

5 If you recoup your investment, you lose the money you have invested. ....

6 If you withdraw an offer, you say that you no longer wish to make the offer. ....

12. Choose the correct word or phrase to fill each gap.

bought forward	backdated	backed

1 If a document is .... , its effect starts from a
date before the date when it is completed or signed.

pegs	refinances	devalues

2 If a government .... the currency of a country,
it reduces its value in relation to other currencies.

settles	redeems	refinances

3 If a borrower .... an existing loan, they find
a lender who will replace it with a new loan with different terms.

surrender	float	refinance

4 If you .... an investment such as an insurance
policy, you cash it out before maturity at a penalty.

settled	pegged	laddered

5 If a currency is .... to another currency, or to
gold, its price is fixed in relation to the price of that currency or to gold.

disinvest	hedge	settle

6 To .... in a company is to remove investment
from it.

13. **Rearrange the letters to find words. Use the definitions to help you.**

1 **blebbu** ....
   (a situation in which a type of investment such as housing or stocks
   has prices driven far above actual value by speculators)

2 **wooligdl** ....
   (an intangible asset that reflects the company's reputation and its
   relationship with its customers)

3 **tropolfoi** ....
   (all of someone's investments together)

4 **redvitaiev** ....
   (an investment that depends on the value of something else)

5 **neycosnivl** ....
   (the state of not having enough money to pay your debts)

6 **pootin** ....
   (an agreement or contract that gives someone the right to buy or sell
   a property or shares at a future date)

14. **Put each sentence into the correct order.**

1 and investing / in spotting / in them / he specializes / promising
   startups
   ....
   ....

2 the bank / its reserves to / purchase securities / make loans or /
   can use
   ....
   ....

3 a going concern / the business / and built it up into / she started / from scratch

....
....

4 was agreed by / the plan / the corporation / to expand / the board of directors

....
....

5 international / we are / changes in / commodity prices / very vulnerable to

....
....

6 are implemented by / the money supply / government policies / control of / and interest rates

....
....

15. Complete the sentences by writing one name in each gap.

> **Securities and Exchange Commission**   **Sallie Mae**
> **Federal Reserve**   **International Monetary Fund**
> **Freddie Mac**   **NYSE MKT (formerly AMEX)**

1 .... is a US government corporation that buys and sells loans in order to provide mortgages to homebuyers.

2 The .... is an international agency that tries to promote trade and improve economic conditions in poorer countries.

3 .... is a publicly traded company that provides and trades in student loans.

4 The .... is the US agency responsible for regulating the financial reporting of companies whose stock is publicly traded.

5 .... is the second-largest stock exchange in the US, after the New York Stock Exchange.

6 The .... is the central bank that issues money in the US.

16. For each question, choose the correct answer.

balanced	afloat	secured

1 If a person, a business, or a country has just enough money to pay their debts and continue operating, they stay ....

translation	transfer	return

2 The act of converting one currency into another is called ....

double investing	insider investing	piggyback investing

3 A situation in which a broker repeats a trade on his own behalf immediately after trading for an investor is called ....

cashback	cash-in-lieu	pro rata

4 Payment of cash instead of stock when a stock splits or changes and the shareholder only owns a partial share is known as ....

a contract note   a cashier's check   a promissory note

5 A note that is a written promise to pay a particular sum of money to someone by a particular date is called ....

contango   collateral   depreciation

6 A situation in which the price of a forward or futures contract is trading above the expected spot price when the contract matures is known as ....

17. Match the two parts together.

1 The ACH is

    a the code that identifies a financial institution on a check or transfer.

2 PMI is

    b the interest rate that banks charge each other for large short-term loans.

3 A HELOC is

    c a US government agency that monitors federal credit unions.

4 LIBOR is

    d an additional loan secured by a residence as well as the original mortgage.

5 An RTN is

    e an insurance policy that protects the holder against loss resulting from default on a mortgage loan.

6 The NCUA is

    f an electronic network used by member institutions to process financial transactions between banks in the US.

18. Put each sentence into the correct order.

1   supplies of oil / the global / there are insufficient / economic boom /
to fuel

....

....

2   attempts to / foreign investment / little success / have had / attract

....

....

3   have been / all of his / placed in / financial interests / a blind trust

....

....

4   maker and / a joint venture / the company was / an advertising
agency / between the film

....

....

5   has just / its first ever / issued / the company / profit warning

....

....

6   make home / he claimed / for more people / that subprime loans /
ownership possible

....

....

19. Choose the correct word to fill each gap.

profit   yield   margin

1 The rate of return on a bond if it is held to its maturity date is called its
.... to maturity.

balanced   known   weighted

2 The cost of capital that is adjusted according to the percentages
of debt financing and equity financing is called the
.... average cost of capital.

utilized   employed   withheld

3 The value of a company's assets minus its liabilities is called capital
....

load   fee   charge

4 A charge that an investor pays when they sell shares in a mutual fund,
or when they cancel a life insurance policy is called a back-end
....

trading   bridge   clearing

5 A financial institution that is an intermediary between two trading
firms for securities transactions is called a ....
house.

withheld   retained   drawn

6 The profit that a company does not pay out in dividends, but keeps in
order to reinvest in itself is called .... earnings.

20. Rearrange the letters to find words. Use the definitions to help you.

1 **ailbotu** ....
(the act of providing money to a company or a bank that is failing, in order to keep it from closing down)

2 **mumirep** ....
(the higher price that is paid for a bond that is trading above par)

3 **ydisaribus** ....
(a company that is part of a larger and more important company)

4 **soubn** ....
(an extra amount of money that is paid to shareholders out of profits)

5 **eurnebtde** ....
(an unsecured corporate bond)

6 **deliy** ....
(is the amount of money or profit that an investment produces)

Solutions

Exercise 1
1. **b** square mortgage
2. **a** fence fund
3. **c** hedge bank
4. **d** custodian loan
5. **b** balloon bonds

Exercise 2
1. valuation
2. annuity
3. maturity
4. corporation
5. liquid assets
6. depreciation

Exercise 3
1. **e** they earn as much money as they spend.
2. **d** you sell shares in it to the public.
3. **a** you pay it back in regular payments.
4. **f** you get the principal or cash back from it.
5. **b** you cancel it by changing the amount to zero.
6. **c** you buy a series of them that mature in sequence.

Exercise 4
1. an allocation
2. a demutualization
3. speculation
4. diversification
5. backwardation
6. capitalization

Exercise 5
1. recession
2. merger
3. arbitrage
4. dividend
5. leverage
6. partnership

Exercise 6
1. blue-chip
2. subordinated
3. outstanding
4. Cumulative
5. pro forma
6. Over-the-counter

Exercise 7
1. increases in salaries are not keeping up with inflation
2. the supermarket giant has announced its acquisition of five local stores
3. profit margins on such low cost items remain extremely low
4. the recent selloff of stocks has worried the Federal Reserve
5. we expect the company's figures to improve by the end of the fiscal year
6. many low-paid workers are reliant on high-interest payday loans

Exercise 8
1. knight
2. pill
3. bear
4. horse
5. fishing
6. parachute

Exercise 9
1. broker
2. ticker
3. tracker
4. voucher
5. backer
6. merger

Exercise 10
1. **d** to meet its short-term debts.
2. **f** between bondholders and shareholders.
3. **a** unless it received a $15 million payment.
4. **e** they had invested in the business.
5. **b** extra finance was easy to secure.
6. **c** the base rate charged to customers of commercial banks.

Exercise 11
2. If someone exports commodities, they sell them to another country.
6. If you withdraw an offer, you say that you no longer wish to make the offer.

Exercise 12

1 backdated
2 devalues
3 refinances
4 surrender
5 pegged
6 disinvest

Exercise 13

1 bubble
2 goodwill
3 portfolio
4 derivative
5 insolvency
6 option

Exercise 14

1 he specializes in spotting promising startups and investing in them
2 the bank can use its reserves to make loans or purchase securities
3 she started the business from scratch and built it up into a going concern
4 the plan to expand the corporation was agreed by the board of directors
5 we are very vulnerable to changes in international commodity prices
6 government policies are implemented by control of the money supply and interest rates

Exercise 15

1 Freddie Mac
2 International Monetary Fund
3 Sallie Mae
4 Securities and Exchange Commission
5 NYSE MKT (formerly AMEX)
6 Federal Reserve

Exercise 16

1 afloat
2 translation
3 piggyback investing
4 cash-in-lieu
5 a promissory note
6 contango

Exercise 17

1 f an electronic network used by member institutions to process financial transactions between banks in the US.
2 e an insurance policy that protects the holder against loss resulting from default on a mortgage loan.
3 d an additional loan secured by a residence as well as the original mortgage.
4 b the interest rate that banks charge each other for large short-term loans.
5 a the code that identifies a financial institution on a check or transfer.
6 c a US government agency that monitors federal credit unions.

Exercise 18

1 there are insufficient supplies of oil to fuel the global economic boom
2 attempts to attract foreign investment have had little success
3 all of his financial interests have been placed in a blind trust
4 the company was a joint venture between the film maker and an advertising agency
5 the company has just issued its first ever profit warning
6 he claimed that subprime loans make home ownership possible for more people

Exercise 19

1 yield
2 weighted
3 employed
4 load
5 clearing
6 retained

Exercise 20

1 bailout
2 premium
3 subsidiary
4 bonus
5 debenture
6 yield

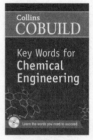

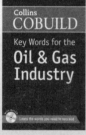